"Embracing challenges that emerge from modern and postmodern culture, gender studies, the natural and human sciences, studies of trauma and violence, and technology, Ross remains convinced that the Christian tradition has wisdom to offer to all those who continue to ponder the meaning of being human. With clarity and grace, she offers a splendid overview of theological anthropology and its contemporary challenges. *Anthropology: Seeking Light and Beauty* is an invitation to join in a lively conversation about the future of humankind in relation to God and to all of creation."

Mary Catherine Hilkert, OP
Professor of Theology
University of Notre Dame

"Professor Ross deftly weaves wisdom from classical Christian sources together with insights from contemporary thinkers to form a tapestry that inspires us to think courageously about what it means to be a human being today. Her commitment to the values of truth and justice is evident throughout, and so are her wide-ranging knowledge, her profound Catholic faith, her esteem for science and the arts, and her engaging style of presentation. This is a splendid text, designed to appeal to a wide range of readers!"

Anne E. Patrick
William H. Laird Professor of Religion and the Liberal Arts, emerita
Carleton College

Other titles in the *Engaging Theology* series:

Engaging Theology: Catholic Perspectives

Anthropology

Seeking Light and Beauty

Susan A. Ross

Tatha Wiley, Series Editor

A Michael Glazier Book

LITURGICAL PRESS
Collegeville, Minnesota

www.litpress.org

A Michael Glazier Book published by Liturgical Press

Cover design by Ann Blattner. Illustration: iStockphoto.

Excerpts from documents of the Second Vatican Council are from *Vatican Council II: The Basic Sixteen Documents*, by Austin Flannery, OP © 1996 (Costello Publishing Company, Inc.). Used with permission.

4   5   6   7   8   9

Library of Congress Cataloging-in-Publication Data

Ross, Susan A.
  Anthropology : seeking light and beauty / Susan A. Ross.
      p.   cm. — (Engaging theology, Catholic perspectives)
  "A Michael Glazier book."
  Includes bibliographical references and index.
  ISBN 978-0-8146-5994-6 — ISBN 978-0-8146-8000-1 (e-book)
  1. Theological anthropology—Catholic Church.   2. Catholic Church—Doctrines.   I. Title.

BT701.3.R68 2012
233—dc23   2012004549

Contents

Editor's Preface

In calling the Second Vatican Council, Pope John XXIII challenged those he gathered to take a bold leap forward. Their boldness would bring a church still reluctant to accept modernity into full dialogue with it. The challenge was not for modernity to account for itself, nor for the church to change its faith, but for the church to transform its conception of faith in order to speak to a new and different situation.

Today we stand in a postmodern world. The assumptions of modernity are steeply challenged, while the features of postmodernity are not yet fully understood. Now another world invites reflection and dialogue, and the challenge is to discover how the meanings and values of Christian faith speak effectively to this new situation.

This series takes up the challenge. Central concerns of the tradition—God, Jesus, Scripture, Anthropology, Church, and Discipleship—here are lifted up. In brief but comprehensive volumes, leading Catholic thinkers lay out these topics with a historically conscious eye and a desire to discern their meaning and value for today.

Designed as a complete set for an introductory course in theology, individual volumes are also appropriate for specialized courses. Engaging Theology responds to the need for teaching resources alive to contemporary scholarly developments, to the current issues in theology, and to the real questions about religious beliefs and values that people raise today.

Tatha Wiley
Series Editor

Preface and Acknowledgments

The more I observed, the clearer it seemed to me that human beings—and I now include myself in that group—are apparently born with, or soon develop, an emptiness, a vacuum, a dead zone at the core of their being.
—Nevada Barr, Seeking Enlightenment . . . Hat by Hat

You have made us for yourself, O God, and our hearts are restless till they rest in You.
—St. Augustine, The Confessions

Defining what being human means is no easy task: embodied spirit, rational animal, body that learns language, hearer of the word, economic actor, person in relationship with God . . . the list can go on and on. Both Nevada Barr, a contemporary mystery writer, and Augustine of Hippo, one of the great Doctors of the Church, say something compelling about our humanity: we are driven by desire. We human beings seek, want, covet, love, ask, and wonder. We chase after something that will make us whole, from the minute we are born until we are no longer able to desire and we die. Sometimes we do this to "fill a hole" that can never be filled. Other times we realize that we wanted something only when we have it in our hands. The lack of desire for food is often a sign that death is near. Desiring is something that has physical and spiritual dimensions. It is necessary to our existence, since if we do not desire to eat, or to be in relationship, we will die. But desire can also lead to despair and death. Desire is both biological and spiritual.

Desire is positive, as Augustine notes above, and it is also negative. The desire for more and more things that American consumer society encourages in us does not lead to happiness.[1] Studies have shown that lottery winners revert to their prewinning state of emotional equilibrium

---

1. See John Kavanaugh, *Following Christ in a Consumer Society: The Spirituality of Cultural Resistance* (Maryknoll, NY: Orbis Books, 2006 [1981]).

within a year after they hit the jackpot. But a lack of desire for anything is a clear sign of depression. This idea of *seeking to fill our emptiness* will be one of the main threads of this extended Christian theological reflection on being human.

Surely human beings seek to fill their emptiness in various ways. As Buddhism sees it, for example, our attachments are the very cause of our suffering; following the way of enlightenment promises a way out of the cycle of death and rebirth. The Christian tradition's understanding is that God is revealed to us in the person of Jesus Christ, whose life, death, and resurrection offer us a way of life and a promise of God's solidarity with us through death and beyond. Even Jesus expressed his desire to be with his friends: "I have eagerly desired to eat this Passover with you before I suffer. . ." (Luke 22:15). A Christian theological anthropology has Christ as its center—a Christ who desires to be with his friends, a God who desires that there be a world in which God's glory can be revealed.

But before exploring further some of the many dimensions of human desires as constitutive of our humanity, it must be said at the beginning of this study that the desires of *all* human beings, especially those who have been denied their basic humanity, must stand as a basic criterion for the adequacy of anything written here. What were the desires of young black men who were lynched for merely looking at a white woman? What are the desires of women who risk their lives for an education? What are the desires of refugees who live in tents because their homes were burned down by their neighbors? What were the desires of our ancestors who may have come to America searching for a better life or who came here in chains? I will try to keep the material context of human desires at the forefront of our considerations as a check against the tendency to assume that a particular set of desires is universally shared, as well as against an overly abstract idea of the human person.

Nor can the nature of our seeking and this emptiness be assumed. Traditional Christian theology has held that human beings (sinfully) desire to "be like God" and thus fall into sin because our desires overtake our rational capacities. Christian feminist scholarship has countered that the desires for power and wealth have historically been the province of men; women have often desired closeness in relationships, sometimes at the expense of their own personhood.[2] Women's desires are often

---

2. See Valerie Saiving (Goldstein), "Human Experience: A Feminine View," *Journal of Religion* 40 (January 1960); and Carol Gilligan, *A Different Voice: Psychological Theory and Women's Development* (Boston: Beacon Press, 1982).

ignored, belittled, or even condemned as demonic—particularly women's sexual desires.[3] Our desires are sometimes not even our own, as Western consumer societies seek to convince us of the many things we did not heretofore realize we "needed."

The title of this book comes from the words of a hymn that I sang often as a student during my five years at the Academy of the Sacred Heart in Grosse Pointe, Michigan. Janet Erskine Stuart, RSCJ (1857–1914), wrote the words to "Spirit Seeking Light and Beauty," a haunting hymn that I have never forgotten. I think that she must have had Augustine's words from the *Confessions* in mind:

> Spirit seeking light and beauty,
> Heart that longest for thy rest,
> Soul that asketh understanding,
> Only thus may ye be blest.
>
> Through the vastness of creation,
> Though your restless heart may roam,
> God is all that you can long for,
> God is all his creatures' home.

Human beings do indeed seek light and beauty, but we end up looking for them, as another song goes, "in all the wrong places." We also seek money, sex, and power, things that nurture us and things that drain us. In his treatise on happiness, Thomas Aquinas lists those things that human beings vainly seek in their pursuit of happiness—wealth, honor, fame, power, bodily pleasure—a list of things that are still sought after in our own time.[4] How can we make sense of our desires in the twenty-first century?

It is no surprise that theological anthropology is one of the most discussed and debated topics in the church today. While texts on the "doctrine of man" were the norm until the 1970s, since then liberation movements, identity politics, and scientific findings, among other factors, have significantly changed the theological-anthropological landscape. Discussions of human nature have become far more complex than in the past. Take, for example, the idea that the human being is a "rational

---

3. See Patricia Beattie Jung, Mary E. Hunt, and Radhika Balakrishnan, *Good Sex: Feminist Perspectives from the World's Religions* (New Brunswick, NJ: Rutgers University Press, 2001).

4. Thomas Aquinas, *Summa Theologiae*, trans. Fathers of the English Dominican Province (Westminster, MD: Christian Classics 1948 [1911]).

animal," the description of the human so often discussed in Catholic theology. Human rationality is not in dispute, at least to this writer, but today we realize it is far more complex, and the lines between human and animal are far more blurry, than was thought until the recent past. In fact, we now know that 96 percent of our genetic makeup is shared with chimpanzees.[5] Scientists have uncovered more and more evidence of "reasoning" in nonhuman animals as diverse as African grey parrots and humpback whales, to say nothing of our primate relatives. So what is it about our particular mode of reasoning that makes us "human"? And even among human beings, how does reasoning take place, and what is the difference between emotion—thought by some ancient and even modern thinkers to bring us closer to nonhuman life—and reason? These are all disputed questions.[6]

Another recent shift in thinking involves questioning what may be termed the image of the "normatively human." The very term "the doctrine of man" suggests that "man," as pictured in Leonardo da Vinci's famous drawing, is male and white. Ancient Western thinkers placed the adult (white) male at the top of a hierarchy, with females, children, and slaves subservient to them. In white, racist societies, men of color shared this lower status, if indeed they were even deemed fully human. Women were thought to lack not only the superior rationality of men but also the capacity to image God as fully as men. Yet biological evidence points to the fact that we are all female before we are male because the human embryo begins life as female. Only when a Y chromosome is activated does the fetus become male. Thomas Aquinas's oft-quoted (and often misunderstood) statement based on Aristotle's metaphysics that women are "misbegotten males" might need, in the face of scientific evidence, to be altered to say that men are "first-begotten females."

A further consideration in recent thinking about the human is an increased emphasis on human bodiliness and sexuality. While the fact that humans are embodied may seem at first to be obvious, the role of the body in Western Christian religious and philosophical thought has often been minimal or even downplayed, with sexuality in particular being that dimension of personhood that is seen to be farthest from the divine. Since human beings' distinctiveness was rooted in their ratio-

5. See Stefan Lovgren, "Chimps, Human 96 Percent the Same, Gene Study Finds," *National Geographic*, August 31, 2005, http://news.nationalgeographic.com/news/2005/08/0831_050831_chimp_genes.html.

6. Daniel Goldman, *Emotional Intelligence* (New York: Bantam Books, 1995).

nality, their embodiment and sexuality were seen as what was shared with "beasts." But more recent Christian thinking has sought to place the body's role in theological anthropology into a more central place, given that the major contention of the Christian faith is that God entered humanity in bodily form. Our notions of humanness inevitably include some sense of the body's place (or its absence), and so to suggest that our embodiment is only ancillary to our humanity is not only wildly mistaken but also contrary to the creedal affirmation of the resurrection of the body.

Yet another issue to note is that of gender and its increased complexity. Is our sexuality and our sexual orientation to others determined genetically? Are we born "gay" or "straight"? What about persons who identify themselves as bisexual or transgendered or who feel that they are born in the wrong sex and change their gender through hormones and/or surgery? Christian theological teaching on sexuality has tended to assume a normative heterosexuality: men ought to be and are attracted to women, and women ought to be and are attracted to men, and this is how God intended things to be.[7] As the saying goes, "God created Adam and Eve, not Adam and Steve." But evidence from evolutionary biology shows that this simplistic answer is woefully inadequate when considering the wide range of both animal and human sexual behaviors. And while magisterial Roman Catholicism holds that same-sex desires are "intrinsically disordered,"[8] the experiences of many people across the spectrum suggest that grace can be found in traditionally unexpected places, including committed same-sex relationships.

A final neglected factor is how we consider the context of our humanity. All of the great philosophers and theologians have assumed a human capacity to think, feel, and act (more or less) freely. That is to say, we take (or do not take) responsibility for our actions, consider how we can affect others, and imagine our futures. But not all people partake fully, or even adequately, in this freedom. Situations of grinding poverty, sociopolitical unrest, or enforced slavery have in the past and still in the present affected how human beings are able to live a *human* life: a life that has the

---

7. See Patricia Beattie Jung and Ralph F. Smith, *Heterosexism: An Ethical Challenge* (Albany, NY: SUNY Press, 1993).

8. Congregation for the Doctrine of the Faith, Letter to the Bishops of the Catholic Church on the Pastoral Care of Homosexual Persons, see especially no. 9, http://www.vatican.va/roman_curia/congregations/cfaith/documents/rc_con_cfaith_doc_19861001_homosexual-persons_en.html.

capacity to reflect the image of God that we all carry, a life that is more than meeting the most basic of human needs. As a number of scholars have argued, theological work will be judged by its adequacy to the experiences of the least among us. So there it must begin.[9]

These considerations will be among the central questions in this book, which seeks to sort out the issues that concern Christian theological anthropology in the early twenty-first century. I make no claim to universality here, and my own limitations as a white, heterosexual, married, childless woman with a privileged educational and social background will no doubt flavor and constrain the discussions in ways of which I will be unaware. This particular theological anthropology comes out of a North American context and may thus reflect the rather individualistic bias of Western culture. Still, my hope is that this book will map the issues involved in thinking about the human in ways that open doors to further discussion and debate.

The structure of this book reflects the method of my own education and the way that I continue to organize my courses. At the University of Chicago Divinity School, where I did my graduate work, seminars typically began with a "review of the tradition." Courses would devote a number of weeks on the great classical, medieval, Reformation, and modern thinkers before plunging into recent scholarship for more current considerations of significant issues like love, hermeneutics, or revelation. I continue to find this a helpful method because it reminds us that many ideas that seem to be very new in fact have a long heritage in the tradition.

The first three chapters constitute this "review of the tradition." I first consider how the biblical witness offers us multiple resources for understanding what it means to be human and also poses many questions that persist into the present. Why did God allow evil to be present in the Garden of Eden? Why does the Bible seem to support unequal treatment of women? As I move into the historical tradition, I comment on how various writers understood the human as image of God, the nature of sin, the desire for knowledge, and the obligations of living a Christian life.

The last four chapters take on some issues that I consider to raise serious questions in the present. They challenge the Christian theologian to consider how a theological anthropology responds to these questions.

9. For an example of this positioning, see Elizabeth A. Johnson, *She Who Is: The Mystery of God in Feminist Theological Discourse* (New York: Continuum, 1992), chap. 12.

If we are living in a "postmodern" age, what does this mean for a Christian understanding of the human person? How does our sexuality express the image of God within us? How do we account for violence and evil? And, finally, how are we to reconcile new developments in science and technology with our theology of the person? Through all of these reflections, the underlying question of the nature of the human and of human desires for God, self, and others remain central.

ᎯᎠᏦ

I wish to express my gratitude to a number of people who have assisted this project. Tatha Wiley, my editor, was both a tireless cheerleader and an astute reader. She made many suggestions and corrections, and she has helped to save me from a number of awkward and erroneous statements. I am also grateful to Hans Christoffersen, my publisher, whose gentle prodding and consistent support meant so much and helped to keep me on track when this project seemed interminable, and to Eric Christensen, whose careful copyediting made this book more readable. I am also very grateful to my graduate assistants, Daniel Dion and Joseph Gulhaugen, who read the manuscript, tracked down countless references, and brought my attention to works of which I was unaware. I would also like to thank Brent Little, whose work on the index is greatly appreciated. Anne Patrick generously read over the entire manuscript and offered many helpful suggestions, and I thank her for her time and friendship. The staff of the Theology Department, Catherine Wolf and Marianne Wolfe, who helped keep many mornings as free as possible and helped with word processing and formatting questions, deserve sustained applause.

While I have been thinking about these issues for a long time, my graduate class in Theological Anthropology in the fall of 2008 was enormously helpful in raising questions and suggesting approaches to the topic, as well as hearing me "try out" a number of the ideas developed in these pages. I am also grateful to so many friends and colleagues who listened to me think through these ideas. Finally, I cannot say enough in thanks to my husband, William George, who read the entire manuscript and made many helpful suggestions, gently pointed out where I was wrong or incomplete, and offered enthusiastic and generous encouragement. I dedicate this book to my students, undergraduate and graduate, over the years, whose questions, corrections, and insights have taught me more than I can say.

Chapter One

Ancient Resources on Being Human

Biblical Resources

Interpreting the Bible

The Christian theological tradition relies on a distinct set of sources for its theological reflection. In the eighteenth century, John Wesley named these four sources: Scripture, tradition, reason, and experience. More recently, David Tracy developed a "method of critical correlation," drawing on both "the Christian fact" and "common human experience."[1] However one describes one's sources, the Christian Bible is fundamental and necessary for theological reflection because the Bible is the Word of God.

But to begin with the Bible is almost immediately to face another problem: How do we use these ancient texts, with their magical stories of talking serpents, their morally problematic stories of God commanding the Israelites to slaughter their enemies, or their edifying stories of self-sacrificial love, as a guideline for understanding the nature of being human? Particularly in the present context of conflicted attitudes toward sexuality, the status of the creation stories, narratives of sexual power and abuse in the Hebrew Scriptures, and Pauline and deutero-Pauline

---

1. On the four sources, or the "Wesleyan quadrilateral," see A. C. Outler, ed., *John Wesley: A Representative Collection of His Writings* (New York: Oxford University Press, 1964). On the method of correlation, see David Tracy, *Blessed Rage for Order: The New Pluralism in Theology* (New York: Seabury Press, 1975).

1

injunctions about sexual mores all make the use of the Bible highly prob-lematic in determining criteria for human moral action and defining what it means to be human.[2] Most mainline Christian denominations approach the scriptural texts from both a critical and an appreciative position. Paul Ricoeur's description of the critical process of reading texts provides a helpful strategy.[3]

There is, to begin, a first naïveté, where one reads or hears the scriptural texts as "literally true" (the world was created in seven chronological days, Moses literally parted the Red Sea, Jesus fed the multitudes with miracu-lously multiplied bread and fish). Such a notion of truth is a simple one, where words mean what they say—nothing more and nothing less. The simple belief of children is often that of a first naïveté, as when children wonder how Santa is going to deliver presents to them when there is no chimney, or how he is going to make it to every house in the world. But biblical literalism is in fact more complex than this childish simplicity. Modern biblical literalism is a response to the challenges of modernity; to wit, how can one reconcile the creation of the world with the scientific evidence of evolution?[4] In contrast to the long tradition of multiple levels of biblical interpretation, a tradition that goes back to the earliest years of Christianity, modern biblical literalism sees "truth" in empirical and verifi-able forms that owe much more to modernity than to the long history of Christian biblical interpretation.[5] The issue of whether fundamentalists are right to think that God created the world in seven days, rather than that the world evolved over millions of years following the massive explo-sion of the "big bang," is much more a question of the human place in the cosmos than of the precise chronology of the divine creative process.

The second moment, the moment of criticism, according to Ricoeur, comes when the evidence of our maturing senses and our intelligence reacts against the mythical and fantastical descriptions of the Bible. It cannot possibly be true that these events happened the way that they are described; such stories collide with all of the evidence and intelligence

2. The term "deutero-Pauline" refers to the consensus by New Testament scholars that some of the letters attributed to Paul were most probably written by his follow-ers; this was a common practice in the ancient world.

3. Paul Ricoeur, *The Symbolism of Evil*, trans. Emerson Buchanan (New York: Harper & Row, 1967).

4. For a fuller development, see Martin Marty and Scott Appleby, eds., The Fun-damentalism Project series, 5 vols. (Chicago: University of Chicago Press, 1994–2004).

5. See, e.g., Sandra M. Schneiders, *The Revelatory Text: Interpreting the New Testament as Sacred Scripture* (Collegeville, MN: Liturgical Press, 1999).

that we have available to us. There is a sense of being deceived, a critical moment when one realizes that one's traditional sources are not to be trusted. Often the response is to reject these biblical accounts as purely mythical, to turn away from religion altogether and embrace scientific evidence, which is empirical and verifiable. But this time of criticism, necessary as it is, can be dealt with in too swift—and indeed, too immature—a way. Such criticism often coincides with adolescence, when clear and unambiguous answers are the desired ones. Once the biblical accounts are uncovered as mythical, one's response may be to reject them altogether as superstitious and incredible. So we need to ask: Is it possible to read these texts in a different way? Surely the stories we know from childhood have deeper meanings!

Over the thirty years of my professional career, all too often I have encountered highly educated colleagues who assume that since I am not only a theologian but also a "practicing" Catholic, I must be a biblical literalist. One of them was stunned to hear that I used Freud in my Introduction to Theology class. Some prospective faculty at our Jesuit, Catholic university still ask if they can teach evolution in our classrooms. Their responses suggest that they agree with Freud, who saw religion as an infantile way of dealing with the terrors of nature and the inevitable disappointments of life. The possibility of a critical but in-depth reading of religious texts has not occurred to many well-educated people.[6] Such a naïve reading of religion is often the result of very bad religious education or no religious education at all.

But with maturity can come a second naïveté, a sense that while these stories may not all be true in the sense of historical facts, they can reveal truth in a far deeper sense. The story of the exodus has been read as a story of God's protection of a persecuted and oppressed group and their emergence into freedom. The parables of Jesus can be read as invitations to enter a world where the meaning of life in the kingdom of God is described in stories that draw on everyday experiences and where expectations are challenged, turned upside down, and transformed. Note as well that this approach to interpreting the Bible rests on a developmental conception of the person: we normally grow in our capacity to understand over time.[7]

---

6. David Tracy, *The Analogical Imagination: Christian Theology and the Culture of Pluralism* (New York: Crossroad, 1981).

7. Ironically, this insight owes a great deal to Freud, who was no friend of religion. See *The Future of an Illusion*, trans. and ed. James Strachey (New York: W. W. Norton, 1989 [1961]).

This capsule description of the critical process, relying on Ricoeur, does not do justice to the complexities of biblical criticism, with its painstaking reconstruction of biblical texts using the scholarly tools of form and redaction criticism, with literary criticism parsing the nature of ancient literary forms, and with the archeological work that has made the ancient texts come alive and revealed the significance of geographical locations. The reader interested in a more thorough introduction to biblical criticism is best advised to seek other sources.[8] My point in this brief excursus into Ricoeur's ideas is to provide a rough outline of how one can find meaning in ancient texts that do not meet the modern criteria of historical veracity, since they are not "historical" works, but which still have powerful meaning for what it is to be human. What are some ways of reading these ancient texts that can shed light on our humanity, even in the present?

Some Biblical Narratives

The ancient Genesis narrative story of Adam, Eve, and the serpent[9] tells a story that most of us learned as children: the first human couple disobeyed God's command that they not eat of the tree of life and were sent permanently out of Paradise. Since then, all humans have suffered the consequences. "In Adam, we all fell." But a closer reading of the story raises all sorts of questions. Why are there two stories, the first with the man and woman being created simultaneously (Gen 1:1–2:4a) and the second with the woman created from the rib of the man (Gen. 2:4b-25)? The man and the woman are described as being "in the image and likeness of God"; in what dimensions do we most resemble our Creator? If Paradise was so perfect, what was the serpent doing there? And why would God have issued this odd command? The story also tells us something about the desires of these archetypal people. The man desires a companion, for the animals are not suitable as friends. The woman sees the tree as "desirable for gaining wisdom" (Gen 3:6). And, as they are expelled from Paradise, part of the woman's punishment is described by God: "your urge shall be for your husband, / and he shall be your master" (Gen 3:16).

Surely the author(s) of this text saw human desire as a very mixed blessing. On the one hand, being able to recognize beauty, as the woman did in seeing what the tree had to offer, is a good thing. And desiring

---

8. See Schneiders, *The Revelatory Text*.
9. See Elaine Pagels, *Adam, Eve, and the Serpent* (New York: Random House, 1988).

wisdom seems to be a good thing as well. But on the other hand, it seems that their desire outreached itself and led to their downfall. Was their desire the problem? If the real issue was disobedience, what was the author's point in deliberately putting the tree off-limits and thus setting the first couple up for temptation? Surely God's intent was not to create unthinking robots, doing only what they were told, or maliciously to place temptation in the midst of their otherwise happy and untroubled lives. So there is a deeper mystery in this story, a mystery that has to do with who we are, what gives us life, and where we are going. Something went amiss, the narrator tells us, and all of humanity suffers the consequences.[10]

The following story in Genesis (Gen 4:1-16) of Cain and Abel receives far less attention than the Adam and Eve narrative. But it too is a significant story because of its focus on fraternal relations and the first murder. Like the preceding story, this one raises questions of its own. Why was Cain's offering seen as lesser than Abel's? Why was Cain banished but then protected by God? No real answers are given in the text, although some commentaries suggest that the younger son Abel is akin to other younger sons (e.g., Jacob and Isaac) who fare better than their elder siblings.[11] God's response to Cain's "insolence"—"Am I my brother's keeper?" (Gen 4:9)—is one of both justice (banishment from tilling the soil) and mercy (protection through his "mark"). The inheritance from their parents is one of a world fractured by relationships of jealousy and pain.

The American writer Jane Smiley's 1989 novella *Good Will* is a powerful retelling of the Genesis story of Adam and Eve.[12] Bob, a Vietnam veteran, and his wife, Liz, have decided to live "off the grid" in rural Pennsylvania, where they are raising their son, Tommy. Bob prides himself on his ability to make a living with almost no money—he tells a newspaper interviewer that his income in the previous year was $342.93. He and Liz raise livestock, grow nearly everything they eat, and live in a house that Bob himself designed and built. They live in "paradise," as the reporter comments. But there is a serpent in this paradise, even though it does not come in the form of a snake. Seemingly out of the blue, and to Bob and Liz's astonishment, their son, Tommy, displays racist and violent behavior. As the story proceeds, the reader learns more

10. See Marjorie H. Suchocki, *The Fall to Violence: Original Sin in Relational Theology* (New York: Continuum, 1994).

11. See Raymond E. Brown, Joseph A. Fitzmyer, Roland E. Murphy, eds., *New Jerome Biblical Commentary* (Upper Saddle River, NJ: Prentice Hall, 1999), 13.

12. Jane Smiley, *Ordinary Love and Good Will: Two Novellas* (New York: Knopf, 1989).

about Bob's desire to control everything about his wife's and son's lives. Against Bob's wishes, his wife wants to worship with a local church. His son recoils at the slaughter of the lambs they have been raising, suggesting an echo of the Cain and Abel narrative. Bob is frustrated and angry with both of them. In the end, Tommy's violence is their undoing, as a fire that he sets leads to the loss of their home and their whole world. They are expelled from their paradise by the forced sale of their farm and come to live like "normal" people: in a rented apartment, with jobs, school, even television. At the end of the story, Bob wistfully comments, "Let us have fragments." Let the tragedies of their lives and the small joys of their new life "lie together" in this new, less-than-perfect life. As he considers "the vast, inhuman peace of the stars" alongside "the smaller, nearer, but not too near human peace" of the small town near his farm, he comes to realize that Paradise has indeed been lost, but there is now a knowledge and wisdom that has been gained from his life.[13]

Smiley's retelling of the Genesis narrative, set in the twentieth century, helps us to see the depth and complexity of the original story. Typically, we learn the Genesis narrative as a story of simple disobedience: the man and the woman were given a command, they violated it, and they paid for it. But such a simple reading skirts away from the many questions that arise. The mystery of this story—why we are the way that we are, why we hide from God, why we are at odds with each other—remains, and we see in Smiley's story how the echoes of this ancient tale of talking snakes and eating fruit takes on a new voice in experiences that we see every day.[14]

Being human is indeed a mystery, and the Genesis story opens up a number of questions and issues. As we will see here and in later chapters, simplistic ideas of human goodness or of our tendencies toward evil are not only wrong but also harmful. To assume, for example, that all of one's students will always come to class, do their assignments on time, and never, ever cheat is, at least to this veteran of over thirty years in the classroom, hopelessly naïve. Yet to assume the worst is also to set up a recipe for disaster: a teacher who has no hopes or dreams for her students will have a very unhappy and unsuccessful experience. The best teachers I know are idealistic but also realistic. They set high standards yet are also careful that assignments or tests are not occasions of temptation. They are

13. Ibid., 196–97.
14. See, e.g., Phyllis Trible, "Eve and Adam: Genesis 2-3 Reread," in *Womanspirit Rising: A Feminist Reader in Religion* (New York: Harper & Row, 1979), 74–83.

clear but also flexible. Biblical wisdom on the human situation seems also to recognize the ambiguity of our existence, even as it still reveals its own patriarchal and hierarchical views of human relationships.

Fragmentation is one of the metaphors that has been used to describe the human situation in the present, with the loss of the certainty of the "modern" world. Our postmodern situation does not offer us the security of stable selves or a stable society. But this fragmentation is something that has much biblical witness as well. So many of the biblical stories are ambiguous and incomplete and leave the reader with a host of questions.

Consider, for example, the story of Jephthah and his nameless daughter (Judg 11). While this story is surely a prime example of a biblical "text of terror,"[15] Jephthah's own history is also a tragic one. Thrown out of his house because of his "illegitimate" birth, Jephthah, like so many rudderless young men, joins a gang and becomes known for his fighting skills. Later, he is hired by the elders of Gilead—the community that had rejected him—to help them defeat the Ammonites. The text tells us that "[t]he spirit of the Lord came upon Jephthah" (Judg 11:29), indicating that Jephthah would be victorious. But not trusting this sign, Jephthah makes a vow to God that he will sacrifice "whoever comes out of the doors of my house to meet me when I return in triumph from the Ammonites" (Judg 11:31). Inevitably, it is his own daughter who greets him and who is ultimately sacrificed so that Jephthah can fulfill his vow. While his daughter's death is the tragic climax to this horrifying story, Jephthah's own background as a social outcast cannot be ignored.

Like the Genesis narrative, this text raises a host of questions. Why did Jephthah make such a foolish and unnecessary vow? Was his daughter aware of this vow? Who and where was her mother? Why was there no rescue call from God for this innocent child, as there was when Abraham was commanded to sacrifice his son Isaac, to stop this violent act and provide an alternative? Jephthah finds himself rejected by society through no fault of his own; perhaps it is his own insecurity that drives him to this feat of braggadocio. The context is already tragic, and even after the terrible sacrifice of his daughter's life, forty-two thousand Ephraimites were later murdered. Was this all due to Jephthah's desire to belong or to show those who had rejected him that he would nevertheless triumph? We do not know the answer to these questions, but both Jephthah's misguided desires and his daughter's desire to please

---

15. Phyllis Trible, *Texts of Terror: Literary-Feminist Readings of Biblical Narratives* (Philadelphia: Fortress Press, 1984).

her father, both of whom are inheritors of a patriarchal culture, lead to unnecessary and violent death.

Gender dynamics play a role in these stories. The author of the Genesis narrative describes the woman's punishment as subjection to her husband—a point that has been used for thousands of years to justify the continued subordination of women to men. The woman's curiosity and desire have been interpreted to mean that she was weaker and more vulnerable to temptation than the man, particularly by New Testament writers like Timothy (cf. 1 Tim 2:9-15). In the story of Jephthah and his unnamed daughter, we are told that she and her companions spent three months "mourning her virginity," since she would never bear children— the main source of a woman's identity in that culture. And in other biblical narratives, we are given what many have interpreted to be divine authority to treat women badly. Renita Weems writes powerfully of the ways that the prophetic tradition described Israel in the language of harlotry, suggesting that women's infidelity is the prime example of Israel's infidelity to God.[16] These are stories written by men and for men, and the examples the writers used show their androcentric perspective.

Nevertheless, there are also positive resources for a more egalitarian view of gender relations in the Bible. The first Genesis narrative, where male and female are created simultaneously, and Paul's statement in Galatians that there "is neither Jew nor Greek, there is neither slave nor free person, there is not male and female" (3:28) have provided biblical interpreters a warrant for an understanding of humanity that emphasizes what women and men have in common. And feminist biblical interpreters have found a wealth of resources for a highly complex and often surprisingly positive view of women's capacity to image God, many of which are seldom quoted or even remembered.[17]

Slavery is another topic with ambiguous biblical resources. For most of human history, slavery has been an accepted social institution. Hagar, Sarah's slave, was actually the mother of Abraham's first son, but as slaves, neither she nor her son, Ishmael, enjoyed the privileges or protection of her relationship with the patriarch Abraham. In the nineteenth

---

16. Renita J. Weems, *Battered Love: Marriage, Sex, and Violence in the Hebrew Prophets* (Minneapolis: Fortress Press, 1995).

17. Also see Elisabeth Schüssler Fiorenza, *In Memory of Her: A Feminist Theological Reconstruction of Christian Origins* (New York: Crossroad, 1995); and Carol A. Newsom, *The Women's Biblical Commentary*, expanded ed. (Louisville, KY: Westminster John Knox Press, 1998).

century, advocates for slavery cited the Bible as a reason for the continuation of the practice of owning (to say nothing of abusing, selling, or killing) human beings. In the New Testament, Paul tells Philemon to return to his master, and while Paul enjoins this master to treat Philemon fairly, interpreters have pointed out that Paul does not question the social structure that supports this (Phlm 1:13).

So in what ways do these narratives tell us what it means to be created "in God's image"? We are given no one clear answer. In the modern context, some scholars have maintained that it is because of God's giving "dominion over the fish of the sea, the birds of the air, and all the living things that move on the earth" and God's exhortation to humans to "[b]e fertile and multiply" and to "fill the earth and subdue it" (Gen 1:28) that Christianity bears the most blame for the ecological crisis.[18] As the "image of God," Israelite kings exercised their power in morally questionable ways. Thus the biblical tradition as a resource for human dignity is again revealed as an ambiguous one: "Slaves, obey your human masters in everything" (Col 3:22); "Wives should be subordinate to their husbands as to the Lord" (Eph 5:22). Do we consider these *God's* words to humanity? Or are these simply human words from an ancient culture struggling to maintain power and the status quo? The fact that these passages are still debated thousands of years after their composition attests to their continuing power.

Jesus as Exemplar

For Christians, the ultimate model of what it means to be human is found in the person of Jesus of Nazareth (recognized as the Christ, the Messiah and Savior of the world) and in the affirmation that Jesus is God with us in the flesh. Interpretations of the significance of Jesus' life and death have, of course, reflected what humans have valued over the centuries.[19] Jaroslav Pelikan's classic study provides a host of names and titles for Christ that are also models for human life: the Rabbi, the Bridegroom of the Soul, the Universal Man, the Poet of the Spirit, the Teacher of Common Sense, the Liberator. There are also titles for Jesus that focus more on his divinity: the King of Kings, the Cosmic Christ, the Prince of Peace. Early Christian debates on Jesus—his suffering, his death, and his role as Savior of humanity—concerned the relationship between his

---

18. Lynn White, "The Historical Roots of Our Ecologic Crisis," *Science* 155 (March 10, 1967): 1203–7.

19. Jaroslav Pelikan, *Jesus Through the Centuries* (New York: Perennial Library, 1987).

divine and human natures and sometimes led to interesting observations and questions about Jesus' humanity. To what extent did Jesus know of his mission? Was Jesus ever sexually aroused? Did he have all of the normal bodily functions of a human being, even the ones that are not mentioned in polite company? How did his divinity affect his humanity? For Christians in the two millennia since his life and death, the task of "following Christ" and living a life in imitation of Christ has been a constant theme.

Contemporary biblical scholarship on Jesus has been a controversial area, raising questions about Jesus that some find troublesome or even blasphemous. The "Jesus Seminar" has focused on what can be most firmly grounded in the historical tradition and thus traced back to Jesus himself. Miracle stories and anything related to the supernatural have been largely dismissed by some modern scholars.[20] Sallie McFague's summary of Jesus' mission as "destabilizing, nonhierarchical, and inclusive" has been picked up by some scholars as representing core aspects of Jesus' message.[21] Since Christology is an issue in and of itself, and is the subject of another text in this series,[22] I will not treat it extensively here but rather indicate how interpretations of Jesus along particular themes have played a central role in understandings of what it means to be human.

The story of Jesus' life and death evokes both positive and negative responses. What it says about how we are to live our lives is not as clear as one may think. The nineteenth-century philosopher Friedrich Nietzsche was highly critical of what he saw as the weakness of Jesus' humanity and argued that Christianity encouraged passivity in the face of challenges to humanity.[23] Some contemporary responses to the significance of Jesus emphasize his "macho-masculinity" in an effort to encourage more male participation in Christianity.[24] For our purposes here, I

20. Cf. Robert W. Funk and the Jesus Seminar, eds., *The Acts of Jesus: The Search for the Authentic Deeds of Jesus* (San Francisco: HarperSanFrancisco, 1998); see also Luke Timothy Johnson, "The Jesus Controversy," in *America* 203, no. 3 (August 2, 2010): 10–13.

21. Sallie McFague, *Models of God: Theology for an Ecological, Nuclear Age* (Philadelphia: Fortress Press, 1987).

22. Gerard S. Sloyan, *Jesus: Word Made Flesh* (Collegeville, MN: Liturgical Press, 2008).

23. Friedrich Nietzsche, *On the Genealogy of Morals*, trans. Walter Kaufmann and R. J. Hollingdale (New York: Vintage Books, 1967).

24. Molly Worthen, "Who Would Jesus Smack Down?" *New York Times*, January 6, 2009, reports on the so-called cussing pastor, Mark Driscoll, whose sermons portray Jesus not as a "wimp, or . . . a gentle man embracing children and cuddling lambs,"

would emphasize the following points. First, Christians have found a model for life in the person of Jesus, particularly in his self-sacrificing love as it led to his death, as it has been interpreted over two millennia.[25] From the second-century instructional writings like *The Didache* to the late medieval work *The Imitation of Christ* to the contemporary bumper-sticker slogan "What Would Jesus Do?" Christians have found in Jesus a paradigm for how to live an upright life. However one's life is ultimately lived out, faithful Christians see in Jesus a pattern for living that serves as a guide to their own lives. This, of course, takes many forms. Jesus can be seen as a model for business leadership,[26] a monk, or a martyr, as well as a model of self-giving love. Somehow, Jesus is always at the center of a Christian theological anthropology; who he is suggests who we ought to be.

Second, Jesus models right relationship with God. The prayers that Jesus said and taught, his openness to God's will, and his awareness of God's presence in everyday life all serve as ways to live and relate to the divine. Jesus' complete openness to God, whom he addressed with the intimate term "Abba," provides a model for the spiritual life, where a person strives to live out this openness to God's will.

Third, Jesus' attitude toward his culture and the world around him sets up a number of questions for later Christians. How should a Christian regard civil government? ("[R]epay to Caesar what belongs to Caesar" [Matt 22:21].) How should a Christian regard wealth? ("[I]t is easier for a camel to pass through the eye of a needle than for one who is rich to enter the kingdom of God" [Matt 19:24].) One's family? ("I have come to set . . . / a daughter against her mother" [Matt 10:35].) War and peace? ("I have come to bring not peace but the sword" [Matt 10:34].) Gender relations?

and who stresses rather a hypermasculine Christ. Worthen goes on to report on how this exemplifies a wider movement in the United States. See also Brandon O'Brien, "A Jesus for Real Men," *Christianity Today*, April 18, 2008, http://www.christianity today.com/ct/2008/april/27.48.html.

25. The issue of the death of Jesus as self-sacrificial, perhaps commanded by an overbearing Father, has been a topic of discussion among feminist scholars in recent years. Cf. Rita Nakashima Brock, *Journeys by Heart: A Christology of Erotic Power* (New York: Crossroad, 1988), 53–57; and Joanne Carlson Brown and Rebecca Parker, "For God So Loved the World?" in *Violence against Women and Children*, ed. Carol J. Adams and Marie M. Fortune (New York: Continuum, 1995), 36–59.

26. See, e.g., Charles C. Manz, *The Leadership Wisdom of Jesus: Practical Lessons for Today*, 2nd ed. (San Francisco: Berrett-Koehler Publishers, 2009); and Ken Blanchard and Phil Hodges, *Lead Like Jesus: Lessons from the Greatest Leadership Role Model of All Time* (Nashville, TN: Thomas Nelson, 2006).

(See Jesus' divorce statements in Matt 5:31-32.) As is obvious from these examples, there is no clear and unambiguous message that we can take from Jesus' pronouncements on the world around him. Jesus was both a part of his own culture and also a critic of some of its practices. While Jesus is indeed a touchstone for Christian theological anthropology, there is no simple way to develop what this message means, as we shall see. What was central for Jesus was life in the kingdom (*basileia*) of God: a kingdom that is in direct contrast to the empire of Rome, that is at work within us and in the way we live our lives, that is not of this world but nevertheless enjoins us to disregard the social norms that keep certain people on the margins (the Samaritan woman, the man who was cared for by the "Good" Samaritan, lepers, adulterers, tax collectors) and to live the radical message of God's overflowing love for all regardless of status. Jesus was skeptical of imperial power and all of its trappings, but he also enjoyed a good meal with friends. In sum, Jesus is the biblical criterion for theological anthropology: in the Christian tradition all understandings of what it means to be human must reckon with his life and his message.

Paul

The first theologian of the Christian Scriptures, the apostle Paul, interpreted his own experience of the risen Christ as the community of Jesus' followers grew, and his reflections on his experience have had a powerful influence on Christian thinking about humanity. Paul's language and concepts were developed out of his Greek educational and cultural background and provided a new way of expressing the message of the itinerant Jewish preacher. As an educated Hellenistic Jew, Paul had absorbed the categories of Greek thought that made distinctions between the soul and the body, between the spirit and the flesh—distinctions that were largely uncharacteristic of the Jewish tradition.[27] These ways of talking about being human have had an enormous staying power into the present. Paul's suggestion that continence is superior to marriage (1 Cor 7:31-32) is one of the most often-quoted phrases that suggest that our sexuality keeps us from being closer to God. Paul's dialectic of spirit and flesh, drawn from his Hellenistic education and context, has sometimes been interpreted to mean that our material and embodied lives are ultimately insignificant in the light of Christ. In the following pages, we will explore further dimensions of this dualism of body and soul.

---

27. Cf. James G. D. Dunn, *The Theology of Paul* (Grand Rapids, MI: Eerdmans Publishing, 1998), 51–78.

Paul's writings on the conduct of women in the early church are particularly significant, as they have been understood to provide norms for the later church. How do we interpret Paul's words in Galatians 3:28 about religion, slavery, and gender, mentioned above? While much feminist scholarship sees this passage as reflecting the egalitarian basis of the very early Christian community,[28] later writings attributed to Paul (a common technique in ancient writings) declare that women should keep silent in church, wear head coverings as a sign of their submission, and find their identity in obedience to their husbands (1 Tim 2:11-12). Not so long ago, the Southern Baptist Convention used these passages to argue against women's leadership, despite the fact that Paul refers often to the many women whom he identifies as coworkers. And while Paul declares that being a follower of Christ entails freedom from the law, his own social location as a Roman citizen and a Jewish convert to the Jesus movement inevitably color his views on gender.

Paul's dialectic of spirit and flesh, taken from his Hellenistic context, raises further questions later connected with body/soul dualism. Did Paul write this way because he anticipated the end of the world in his own lifetime? How does the conflict of spirit and flesh inform the profoundly incarnational message of the life of Jesus and the message that he preached?

In sum, biblical sources for theological anthropology are rich, complex, ambiguous, and even contradictory. For centuries, people who considered themselves "good Christians" used the Bible to justify the practice of slavery and the domination of women. The Bible is still used to support capital punishment, the condemnation of same-sex relationships, and the subordination of women. Also fundamental to the biblical tradition are recurring themes of the human desire for God, God's desire for human beings, and the many ways that these desires intersect and collide with each other.

Early Christianity on Being Human

Christian theology makes a distinction between the canonical Scriptures, which are inspired by God and thus have priority as revelation, and tradition, which is the record of the church as it responds to issues over the years and which has come to reflect the received wisdom and

---

28. See Schüssler Fiorenza, *In Memory of Her.*

shared faith of the Christian community. Tradition, in the sense that I will be using the term, refers to the texts and figures that have attained authoritative status in the church. At some point in the first two centuries after the death and resurrection of Jesus Christ, the early church made some decisions about what constituted "Scripture" and what constituted the ongoing teaching and learning of the church. And much of what determined what was to be authoritative emerged from controversies concerning the very meaning of the Christian message. As Christianity spread into the Mediterranean world, it encountered a number of religious movements and ideas about the human that it could not ignore. Some of these movements were incorporated into Christianity in various ways; others continued to pose questions about the Christian message. All of them raise significant issues for theological anthropology.

Gnosticism, Irenaeus, and Early Christian Martyrs

When we turn to some of the first Christians who wrote on human nature, one of their main challenges was answering Gnosticism, a philosophy of life that is deeply suspicious of desire. One could venture to say that Gnosticism is a way of thinking about life that is found in nearly every period of time. Gnosticism—from the Greek word for knowledge, *gnōsis*—is about possessing the necessary and secret knowledge for salvation. Gnosticism tends to see the world in polarized terms (spirit versus matter) and is deeply suspicious of the flesh. It was a concern for early Christian writers because of the ways that it affected both Christology and theological anthropology.

Gnostics believed that human beings in their present state had fallen from a previous condition of beatitude and spirit and that our present existence in mortal flesh is the tragic result of this fall.[29] Thus, Jesus the Christ, as divine, could not have been fully human, since that would mean that he shared in the sinfulness and mortality of the human race—unthinkable for the divine! Therefore, in response to Gnostics, early Christian authors took great pains to emphasize the humanity of Jesus: that he truly was born of a woman, lived a human life, suffered, died, and was raised by God. But the Gnostic phenomenon is one that has recurred many times in human history; it expresses a deep tension between flesh and spirit. As Paul notes, to be "of the flesh" (1 Cor 3:3) is not a good thing, while at the same time he and others recognize that

---

29. See Peter Brown, *The Body and Society: Men, Women, and Sexual Renunciation in Early Christianity* (New York: Columbia University Press, 1988).

the fact that embodiment is a gift from God—"Therefore glorify God in your body" (1 Cor 6:20). Human beings need ways of navigating this difficult relationship, and Gnosticism was one way of providing the necessary knowledge for doing this.

Ancient Gnosticism took different forms: one held that material reality was of so little significance that human beings could do whatever they wanted with their bodies, so sexual licentiousness was tolerated. What did it matter what one did if the body was in truth inconsequential? The other form held that the only way out of human entrapment in material reality was through rigorous asceticism. Although their methods were different, both forms shared a fundamental disgust with human embodiment, particularly in its "lowest" forms. Such a perspective, early Christians realized, was profoundly contradictory to the most basic tenet of Christian belief: the incarnation in which God takes on flesh, suffers, and dies.

Irenaeus of Lyons (d. ca. 202) was the earliest and most articulate spokesperson for the goodness of enfleshed humanity, and his oft-quoted maxim "The glory of God is [the human being] fully alive" sums up Christianity's rootedness in human embodiment.[30] To be human is to grow, change, and eventually die, but Irenaeus did not see these processes as inherently flawed or evil. Growing and maturing are essential dimensions of being human. For Irenaeus, human experience is key. God did not create us like angels, who know everything at once; rather, we "slowly progress" and learn from our experiences, as Thomas Aquinas will later concur.[31] Our very humanity is a work in progress. Human beings need to realize and accept what it means to be human. "We, however, complain that instead of being made gods from the beginning, we are first human and then divine."[32] Irenaeus's sense that human growth and development is both good and intended by God is very significant and will be a theme picked up by many later Christian theologians; it was extraordinarily important that such an articulate spokesperson for the goodness of creation and of the body was there for Christianity in its early years.

While Gnosticism per se is arguably no longer the main threat to Christianity in the present, it is worth reflecting on the stubborn

---

30. Irenaeus, *Against the Heresies* IV.XX.7.

31. Thomas Aquinas, *Summa Theologiae* I, qq. 50–64 and qq. 106–14.

32. Irenaeus, *Against the Heresies*, in J. Patout Burns, ed., *Theological Anthropology* (Philadelphia: Fortress Press, 1981), 25.

persistence of antimaterial ideas in Christian history. Whereas Christianity's main assertion is that God has come to dwell with humanity in the flesh, the superiority of the "soul" over the body is often simply assumed.

In the first three centuries of Christianity, Gnosticism and related issues, such as whether or not the God of creation and the God of salvation were the same, were the major ideas under debate. Waves of persecution by imperial Rome were followed by periods of tolerance, as Christianity developed its own distinctive identity in relation to its Jewish heritage, affirmed its continuity with Judaism by including the Hebrew Scriptures (as the "Old" Testament) in its canon of sacred texts, and sought to understand the Word of God. In those uncertain times, the more complex questions of how the humanity of Jesus could coexist with his divinity would have to wait for fuller debate until the fourth and fifth centuries when things were religiously and politically calmer. In those early years, the martyrdom of many Christians in these sporadic persecutions (the Greek word for "martyr" literally means "witness") resulted in a new way of living the Christian life: as followers of Jesus in the highest sense. In the words of Elizabeth Johnson, "martyrs are the ideal disciples because they follow Jesus Christ even to his death on a cross."[33] Women and men, young and old, clergy and lay, all could and did become martyrs. And as Maureen Tilley observes, "asceticism logically and practically preceded martyrdom. In fact, it made martyrdom possible."[34] Rigorous practices of self-denial trained the early Christian martyrs for their later trials. Martyrdom was something that both women and men experienced and offered role models for women and men of later centuries.

Asceticism

Once the anti-Christian persecutions ended in the early fourth century, asceticism took on some new forms, as the threat of martyrdom no longer provided a context or rationale for its practice. Asceticism, a form of rigorous self-discipline, had always been one option for ancient religious traditions; certainly John the Baptist provides one significant example, as do the Essenes, a very strict Jewish sect, in a context where the significance of the body was contested. Heavy taxation, oppressive government, and

---

33. Elizabeth A. Johnson, *Friends of God and Prophets: A Feminist Theological Reading of the Communion of Saints* (New York: Continuum, 1998), 73.

34. Maureen Tilley, quoted in Johnson, *Friends of God and Prophets*, 72.

the countercultural themes of the Christian message—where providing children for the fatherland was not the highest ideal—served as justification for withdrawing from the world and living a life of renunciation of desires.[35] For women, foregoing marriage and children meant that they could live lives of prayer and devotion and enjoy a kind of independence not possible in the traditional patriarchal household. For men, the ascetic life also meant avoidance of military service and the heavy responsibilities associated with being the paterfamilias. The point to be made here is that asceticism is a complex practice that comes not only from devotion but also from a social, economic, and political context where living ascetically may at the time appear to be more attractive and even more practical for many reasons.[36] While asceticism is a thread that still winds its way throughout the Christian tradition, its focus on disciplining the body will always, in some way, be a response to how the body is understood in a given historical context.

The value of asceticism is a theme that will recur often in the Christian tradition's reflections on being human. Although the Nicene Creed proclaims belief in the resurrection of the body, signifying its goodness by pointing to its future glorification by God, some, even today, hold that what is most truly human is our soul or spirit, with the body coming in a distant second place. Our human desires for food, sex, and pleasure are thus continually suspect, and the ascetic impetus seeks to dampen those desires, if not extinguish them entirely. This debate played out in ancient discussions of the value of marriage. Jovinian (d. ca. 405) argued that marriage was equal to virginity as a calling from God, but he was roundly condemned by his peers, especially Jerome. Jesus, of course, was assumed to be a virgin (as far as we know, or as tradition has always held), as was his mother Mary, although the complexity of the meaning of "virginity" in the ancient world is seldom given adequate attention.[37] And while ascetic practice in the present is usually associated with the denial of sexual desires, in the ancient world the focus was more often on quelling one's desire for food.[38]

Any discussion of asceticism must also contend with the misogyny that is another thread—in this case, a poisonous one—running through

---

35. For a rich treatment of this theme, see Brown, *The Body and Society*, 108–9.

36. See Brown, *The Body and Society*, especially chap. 11.

37. See Jane Schaberg, *The Illegitimacy of Jesus: A Feminist Theological Interpretation of the Infancy Narratives* (San Francisco: Harper and Row, 1987).

38. Brown, *The Body and Society*, 219.

the Christian tradition. By no means is Christianity alone in its misogyny.[39] But its focus on a celibate, male savior, born of a virgin mother, and the development of a community that for many reasons, including misogyny, excluded—and continues to exclude—women from its official leadership led to implications that were overwhelmingly negative for their focus on women's inherent sinfulness. Tertullian's claim that women are the "devil's gateway," passages in the New Testament that women are responsible for the Fall of humanity, and condemnations of women as closer to evil than men in the medieval witch hunts—these are just some of the many ways that male religious leaders saw women as enemies of the Christian message.[40] In Gnostic literature and also in orthodox spiritual literature, for a woman to "become male" was a positive thing: it meant that she transcended the female flesh that dragged her down and that she was closer to God, as the full image of God was found in men but only secondarily in women. These ideas are, of course, not only wrong but also sinful, since women are created in the image of God as much as are men (Gen1:26-27).

The practice of asceticism poses interesting questions about human desires. Can we, through rigorous acts of self-denial, train our bodies to desire less? Does practicing asceticism make us more in control of ourselves? In the present context, we might consider how the Western (and increasingly global) obsession with thinness as a sign of beauty and of control suggests that the perfect body is simply a question of hard work and self-discipline, and those who are overweight must therefore be lazy and unable to control their appetites.[41] In the ancient world, however, asceticism provided one significant way of showing how human beings

39. Although the book needs to be taken in its context, and the examples need to be seen within their own cultural frameworks, Mary Daly's *Gyn/Ecology: The Metaethics of Radical Feminism* (Boston: Beacon, 1978) provides five powerful examples of misogyny across cultures: foot binding (in China), female genital mutilation (in Africa), widow burning (in India), witch hunting and killing (in Europe and North America), and the practices of gynecology and psychiatry in contemporary Western culture.

40. Gary Macy, "Impasse Passé: Conjugating a Tense Past," *Proceedings of the Sixty-Fourth Annual Convention of the Catholic Theological Society of America* (June 4–7, 2009): 1–20.

41. See Caroline Knapp, *Appetites: Why Women Want* (New York: Counterpoint, 2003). The NBC reality television show *The Biggest Loser* suggests that even the morbidly obese can, through hard physical exercise and rigorous diet control, achieve a close-to-ideal body weight. It is interesting to note that many of the "losers" have regained much of their weight. Cf. Gina Pace, "Life after 'Loser': Every Day Is a Struggle," MSNBC, January 5, 2009, http://today.msnbc.msn.com/id/28449267; and

could improve themselves along the rocky road to salvation. Along with other ancient practices such as Stoicism, an ethical system that preached indifference to desires and passions and with which Christian asceticism has some connections, ascetical practices demonstrated that if human beings could sufficiently discipline themselves, they could overcome, at least in part, their sinful desires. Later, we will see how, with Augustine, the ascetical practices of self-control were decidedly *not* the direct route to salvation, as they suggested that we can achieve it through our own efforts; indeed, the idea that we can "save ourselves" through our own efforts will prove to be one whose time comes back again and again in Christian history, albeit in different forms in different times.[42] Nevertheless, Augustine saw our selfish human desires as most powerfully evident in our sexuality, a theme to which we will return.

Platonism and Origen

Yet another related and significant train of thought in early Christianity related to conceptions of the human person is Platonism in its various forms. Derived from the ideas of the Greek philosopher Plato, Platonism sees rationality as the highest quality of human beings. The person who is truly in the image of God is the one whose desires are under rational control. As a philosophy of life, Platonism predates Christianity; its antiquity provided a justification for its adaptation by Christians, since all that is good comes from God.

Platonism sees the mind or spirit as superior to the body. In a philosophy where men are associated with the mind and women with the body, being female is necessarily inferior to being male. Yet Platonism is not simply another form of Gnosticism. The body is a necessary reality, and when we are fully in control of ourselves, we are also fully in control of our bodies. Our reality here on earth is, to be sure, only a shadow of the higher and more spiritual realities that are above, but this does not mean that our earthly realities are bad—rather, they are lower while at the same time necessary. One scholar of early Christianity defines the influence of Platonism this way: "Christian Platonism identifies the divine image in humanity not as the autonomy of self-determination but

---

"Biggest Loser's Erik Chopoin Faces Weight-Loss Struggle Again," *People*, January 6, 2010, http://www.people.com/people/article/0,,20421574,00.html.

42. See, e.g., Roger Haight, *The Experience and Language of Grace* (New York: Paulist Press, 1979), for his observation on liberation theology and connections with Pelagianism.

as rationality, the human capacity for knowledge of God."[43] Early Christian thinkers who were well-educated in the secular classical tradition found powerful connections between their theological and philosophical education (the ancients did not separate these two fields as we do today) and their Christian beliefs: surely the ancient philosophers were inspired by the same Spirit that inspires Christians! Therefore, the human spirit within us, a spirit that was implanted in us by God, desires union with God and must overcome the obstacles that the body poses. Justin Martyr is known for his "baptism" of the ancient figures of Moses and Plato as being inspired by the same spirit of Christianity.[44]

Christian Platonists understood that humans were created as body and soul and that the proper relationship between them was the superiority of the spirit over the flesh: in Paradise, our bodies were perfectly obedient to the spirit. This point is later echoed in Augustine's vision of sex in Paradise: it would have been perfectly rational and practiced only for the purpose of procreation. But in this life our desire for God is distracted by desire for other things that are lesser than God. As the Genesis 2 story reveals, the first couple allowed themselves to be distracted by such things.

One of the most significant Platonists of the early church is Origen (ca. 185–254). Origen shared the Platonist sense that the body is dragged down by the soul. Peter Brown describes Origen's theological anthropology in typical Platonist language, where "the present human body reflected the needs of a single, somewhat cramped moment in the spirit's progress back to a former limitless identity."[45] Given this situation, abstinence from sex would hasten the person's progress. As the story goes, Origen castrated himself so that he would be freed from the lower urges of his sexuality. Origen's theological anthropology was, interestingly, threefold: the spirit was the highest level, with the soul next as the seat of morality, and finally the body. The body was the unruly member of this trio, and while it was a creation of God, it needed constant supervision.

Augustine

No theological anthropology can take a shortcut around the monumental figure of Augustine (354–430), whose long and powerful shadow over Christian conceptions of self and personhood is unavoidable. Unlike

---

43. J. Patout Burns, ed., *Theological Anthropology*, 7.

44. Justin Martyr, *First Apology*, in *Early Christian Fathers*, ed. Cyril C. Richardson (New York: Macmillan, 1970), 272.

45. Brown, *The Body and Society*, 47.

many other early Christian writers, Augustine shared his life story in his *Confessions*. This book became a template for the Christian story. His voluminous writings defy categorization, and scholars continue to debate his influence on Christian theology.[46] Augustine's story includes many of the influences discussed above, as well as Manicheanism, an elaborate religious tradition with strong Gnostic roots that attracted Augustine in his youth. While he never rose above the lower status of "hearer," he was taken by its system of knowledge. And while he repudiated Manicheanism when he became a Christian, some scholars think its influences remained in his later thought, particularly in his thinking on sexuality. Asceticism, with its concern for disciplining the body, was also important for Augustine. While he is often blamed for helping to develop Christianity's suspicious attitude toward sexual desire, in fact Augustine argued that sexuality was a good created by God. This good had been damaged by the Fall of Adam and Eve, and in our postlapsarian world all of our human desires were tainted by sin.[47]

Desire is at the heart of Augustine's understanding of what it means to be human. His classic statement, quoted in the opening epigraph of this book, holds that all human beings have a desire for God, but this desire is tempted by lesser things and sinfully makes idols of them. The key to our living a Christian life is to love God above all, as well as to love God through the things of this world, never as ends in themselves but always as a means of loving God.[48] There is a strongly Platonist thread running through Augustine's work. Our wills, since the Fall, are no longer free; we cannot save ourselves. Thus, human sinfulness, inherited from our first parents, emerges when our desire gets out of hand, when we seek to satisfy only our lowest urges, and when we give in to them rather than control them. Any freedom that we have is a freedom to choose among the many evils we confront in our lives, and without God's grace we are not free to choose the good.

Augustine's understanding of the limitations of human freedom would continue to be a contested point for successive generations of theologians. In particular, the Reformation thinkers found in Augustine

46. See The Augustinian Moment: Reflection at the Limits of Selfhood conference at the University of Chicago, May 26, 2010. The papers of this conference are published in *The Journal of Religion* 91, no. 1 (January 2011).

47. See Margaret Miles on Augustine for a nuanced reading: *Augustine on the Body* (Missoula, MT: Scholars Press, 1979); or *Desire and Delight: A New Reading of Augustine's Confessions* (New York: Crossroad, 1992).

48. See his *On Christian Doctrine*, especially bk. IV.

the complete and utter reliance on grace—and not on the church or the will of the person—that they saw as central to the Christian message. Later in Augustine's life, his concern about an elevated concept of the freedom of the will took on a zealousness as he attacked Pelagius's conviction that human beings learned sin from their environment and could overcome sin through their own efforts. For Augustine, if we think that we can overcome sin through our own efforts, then what need do we have for God? For the church? For grace?

For Augustine, we are constituted by our desires. Our sexual desires in particular epitomize the ways in which our constant need to satisfy ourselves are played out. Concupiscence, that drive to satisfy the self—in the lingo of Chicago politics, *ubi est meum*? (Where's mine?)—is what constitutes our post-Fall existence, and getting "what's mine" in our sexual fulfillment and pleasure is the issue that haunted Augustine for much of his life. For Augustine, the sin of our first parents was one of concupiscence: Adam and Eve desired something for themselves that was at odds with God's will; concupiscence ultimately finds its paramount expression in sexuality. In and of itself, sex is not bad; as Augustine argues, there was indeed sex in Paradise since it was created by God for procreation. But under the sway of fallen human existence, any and all acts of sex are sinful. The most sinful sexual acts are those that are performed for pleasure alone. Thus, any contraceptive act is done for the pleasure of the person and not for the purpose for which God made it.

For Augustine, then, sexuality is the prime, although not the sole, location for our sinfulness. Sexuality is where our concupiscence rears its ugly head most boldly, and Augustine was keenly aware of this and wrote copiously about it, as he struggled with his own sexuality. But it is worth asking whether or not this focus on self-satisfaction and sex holds true universally. Perhaps it is the case for male sexuality, where desire and physical sexuality join so completely. Put bluntly, for men, without desire there is no erection, no sexual act. But for women, it is not always the case that sexual expression is accompanied by desire. While sexual pleasure and autonomy have taken on great significance for women especially in the global North, sexual abuse, rape, and sexual violence continue to plague women all over the world. In many parts of the world, women have virtually no power of consent to sex. So the long association of sex with sinfulness has a potentially different significance for women than for men. This is not to say that women have no sexual desire! Indeed, one could argue that the phenomenon of women's sexual desire and its expressions has found a voice only in recent years, with the women's movement and the sexual revolution of the late twentieth century. Female sexual desire continues to be seen as a threat to society in some cultures, as the practice of female genital mutilation attests. But it is interesting to note that church teaching has historically paid little if any attention to women's sexual desires and a great deal to men's.

When it comes to Augustine's views on women, we face again another complex set of ideas. Augustine was famously devoted to his mother, Monica, and her centrality in the *Confessions* cannot be overlooked. For many years, Augustine lived with an unnamed woman (his concubine) in a relationship marked by love and fidelity; they had a son together. Such a relationship was common in the ancient world, particularly when marriage to the right person of the right social class was not yet possible. When Augustine decided to live a celibate life, his companion returned to Africa. Yet Augustine believed that women were not the best suited for friendship; he excluded women from his monastic community and he saw women as the weaker sex. Like many thinkers, Augustine's attitude toward women was marked by deep conflict and ambiguity, attitudes that sadly remain alive and well in the present.

Much, much more could be said about Augustine's influences on theological anthropology. For our purposes here, let me highlight the following. First, by the time of Augustine's death, the early church had settled on an attitude toward the body that both recognized its intrinsic goodness and maintained its connection with sinfulness. That is to say, in working through christological doctrines, which by the Council of Chalcedon in 451 maintained that Jesus Christ was "true God and true man," the church had affirmed that the body was a good creation of God. Thus the church had countered, more or less effectively, the Gnostic conviction that the body was an obstacle to salvation.

Second, this affirmation of the body was accompanied by a strong Platonist thread that saw the body as inferior to the soul and therefore in need of discipline. There remained some suspicion of the body, particularly of the sexual body. Ascetic practices were encouraged, and the idea that married life was a lesser choice than the virginal life became more and more prominent. As Peter Brown puts it in his masterful study of the role of the body in early Christianity, by the time of the early Middle Ages, "Christian notions of sexuality had tended to prise the human person loose from the physical world," and thus church leaders "had protected human sacred space from the formless, purely biological, products of the body that periodically reminded the faithful of their indissoluble connection with the physical world."[49]

Third, conceptions of the significance of gender had become more established within Christian teaching. Despite the leadership of women in the very early church, male leadership had become the norm by the second century, and statements about the inferiority of women were more and more frequently proclaimed and even assumed by Christian theologians. Yet despite their relegation to a lower sphere, women continued to make serious contributions to the early church. Vowed religious life, particularly for well-off women, became a refuge from arranged marriages and constant childbearing and a place where one could become educated and reflect on the significance of the Christian life. Holy women served as spiritual advisers to some of the most prominent theologians of the early church and were held up by them as models of piety.

Conclusion

What resources for theological anthropology can be found in this complex mix of biblical narrative and early Christian teaching? Let me suggest several. First, human beings are created in God's image. This is affirmed in both creation stories in Genesis. The first account, in contrast to competing stories in the ancient Mediterranean world, asserts God's direct creation of matter and the inherent goodness of creation. The second offers a narrative of creation as relational: between humans and animals, male and female, humanity and God. It is largely assumed by biblical writers that men are more closely the image of God, but women's virtue and significance, while often challenged, is by no means absent.

Second, there are deep fractures in divine-human and human-human relations—as well as between humans and the nonhuman world, modern commentators would add. Brother kills brother; humans turn their backs on God; nations abandon God for idols, and they capture and even slaughter their enemies as well as their own people; slaves are used and abused and even in the New Testament are admonished to obey their masters; children are unnecessarily sacrificed; women and men are raped. The list of biblical atrocities can go on and on. Let me make clear, however, that this list is no match for the atrocities that continue to plague the world of today. This point is sometimes forgotten by those who

---

49. Brown, *The Body and Society*, 432, 434.

mistakenly view the Jewish tradition as simply "preparation" for the fuller Christian message. Human sinfulness and evil, and God's compassion for us, are well attested in the entire biblical witness, Hebrew Scriptures and New Testament alike.

Third, the Christian tradition struggled and continues to struggle with an ambivalence about the place of the body and sexuality. While Christianity teaches that God became one of us in the flesh, the flesh continues to be seen as the place where we are most prone to sinfulness. Celibacy is still seen as a higher calling than married life, despite the teaching of the Second Vatican Council that *all* Christians are called to the same holiness (*Lumen Gentium* 5).

Fourth, there is a marked ambivalence about women's role in Christianity. While many of the ancient fathers of the church were nurtured and supported by women throughout their lives and counted women among their companions, the role of women remained subordinate to that of men. Certainly, much of this subordination was simply part and parcel of the social context in which they lived. But the genuine contributions of women to the thinking and practice of Christianity were often underplayed, if not ignored.

Finally, the social context of human life played a significant role in ancient Christianity; indeed, much recent scholarship on the New Testament and the early church emphasizes the influence of secular culture. It is important, then, that readers of early church documents see these texts within their context, which is very different than the present. All of these matters touch on human desires: for God, for happiness, for martyrdom, for sexual pleasure. As we move further along in the Christian story, we will see these themes emerge again and again.

Chapter Two

Resources from the Medieval and Reformation Periods

Medieval Thought

Monasticism and Learning

The title of Jean LeClercq's (1911–93) classic text *The Love of Learning and the Desire for God*[1] serves well as a theme for theological anthropology in the Middle Ages. Based on the monastic tradition of spirituality and learning, the book provides a rich picture of monastic life with its focus on both study and prayer (*ora et labora*—"work and prayer"—is the motto of the Benedictines). And while monastic life is not the only model for personhood in this time, its influence on church life and thought is immeasurable. In this first section I will focus on learning and prayer. By "learning" I mean the collection of efforts to understand the human being as rational, and by "prayer" I refer to the way in which the person lives out his or her religious commitments. Focusing on these elements can shed light on the understanding of the human being that emerges in the medieval period. As Leclercq's title indicates, the "love of learning and the desire for God" fits well with our emphasis on the ways that our desires and longings shape our lives.

---

1. Jean LeClerq, *The Love of Learning and the Desire for God: A Study of Monastic Culture*, trans. Catharine Misrahi (New York: Fordham University Press, 1961).

The Middle Ages (roughly from the fifth to fifteenth centuries) have been popularly known as the "Dark Ages," a time following the collapse of the Roman Empire when barbarians roamed Europe and scholarship thrived only in small pockets of civilization called monasteries. To what degree it was truly "dark" for those who lived during this period is something we cannot fully know. We do know, however, that Augustine's suspicion of worldly desires left its mark on this time. Toward the end of his masterpiece on body and sexuality in the early church, Peter Brown writes of the church's thinking on the person and particularly on sexuality in the early Middle Ages: "In the Catholic thought of the early Middle Ages, human flesh emerged as a quivering thing. Its vulnerability to temptation, to death, even to delight, was a painfully apposite concretization of the limping will of Adam."[2] The physicality of human existence was a complex subject for the theologians of the Middle Ages, a time when the fragility of life was a constant and immediate reality. By the time of the "high" Middle Ages, in the twelfth and thirteenth centuries, the development of systematic approaches to theology, such as we find in the *Sentences* of Peter Lombard or Thomas Aquinas's *Summa Theologiae*, led to a highly developed understanding of the person.

Between the time of Augustine and the beginnings of the Reformation period—about one thousand years later—theological understandings of the person underwent significant development. Augustine's influence hangs heavily over the Middle Ages, as the quotation from Brown suggests, but newer ideas also play a significant role, particularly those that emphasize the intellectual capabilities of the human person. During this time, there is something of a theological move away from the body to the mind. To illustrate this, I will first focus on Anselm of Canterbury (1033–1109), whose ideas about the human ability to "think God" and about the nature of salvation will prove to be of great significance for theological anthropology. I will then turn to Thomas Aquinas (ca. 1225–74), whose thought on human nature continues to have a powerful influence, particularly in Catholic theology. Along the way, other thinkers with signal contributions to theological anthropology will also receive mention.

Anselm was a Benedictine monk and later archbishop of Canterbury. While his theology was nurtured and developed in the meditative environment of the monastery, he points to the future with his emphasis on what the mind can do on its own, by thinking and reasoning apart

---

2. Peter Brown, *The Body and Society: Men, Women, and Sexual Renunciation in Early Christianity* (New York: Columbia University Press, 1988), 434.

from, although never wholly separated from, revelation. In this he was unlike most theologians since the time of Augustine, who emphasized knowledge of the Bible. Anselm's *Proslogion*, an intellectual exercise in thinking about the existence of God, reflects his monastic context—he begins with a prayer—and the "love of learning" that was so much a part of monastic life and was soon to grow more intensely in the new universities developing across Europe. Anselm begins this treatise by encouraging readers to set aside their other thoughts and contemplate God, who is, in Anselm's famous formulation, "that than which nothing greater can be thought."[3] It is important that Anselm is careful to note that it is "God who gives understanding to faith."[4] Anselm's definition of God is a kind of theological shorthand that assumes this definition would be acceptable and understandable to any reasonable human person. God is so much higher than the human, so much more that we cannot even conceive of God; if we do, then what we have thought is not God. Further, it is one thing to imagine something and another to understand that it exists. Logically, then, Anselm argues that to exist *both* in the imagination *and* in reality is greater than to exist in the imagination alone. So if God *is* what we believe ("that than which nothing greater can be thought") and *if* we agree that to exist in reality *and* in the imagination is superior than to exist in the imagination alone, then necessarily, God must exist.

Anselm goes on to argue that if we can conceive of something greater than "that than which nothing greater can be thought," then we would automatically be thinking of God, since this is what God is by definition. As he moves through his argument, Anselm further develops his case by saying that God cannot *not* be thought to exist, since God's existence is by definition what Anselm has proposed. In "thinking God" we think of what it is that cannot be thought to be higher. And since thinking, considering our existence, is what we humans do, only God's existence is necessary. All other existence is contingent. Furthermore, given our rational capacity, we are bound to come to this conclusion.[5] Thus the human being is able to come to the same conclusion that faith teaches us!

3. St. Anselm, *Proslogion*, in *The Major Works*, ed. Brian Davies and G. R. Evans (New York: Oxford University Press, 2008), 87.

4. Ibid.

5. See David Burrell, *Exercises in Religious Understanding* (Notre Dame, IN: Notre Dame University Press, 1974), 45–79, for a brief and excellent treatment of Anselm's argument.

All of us can imagine the circumstances in which we came to be and how if something were to occur that would have prevented our parents from meeting each other, we would not even exist at all. In teaching Anselm's argument, I have often used the example of the 1985 film *Back to the Future*, in which the character Marty McFly finds himself in the past and desperately tries to make sure that his parents meet. Since his actions and existence in the past can alter the possibility of his existence in the present (the so-called butterfly effect), he is acutely aware of the possibility that if his parents do not connect, his whole existence will simply disappear. Fortunately, his parents meet and Marty's existence is saved.

Whether or not Anselm's Ontological Argument is in fact successful in making an airtight case for God's existence is not our basic question, although it is a fascinating one, and the reader is encouraged to consult the many resources on this discussion. My point is rather to show Anselm's utter confidence and delight that human reason can *understand* and come to the conclusion of God's necessary existence. Some later theologians, particularly Thomas Aquinas, rejected Anselm's argument, while others, such as Descartes, found this formulation to be a fertile way of considering the logical dimensions of belief in God.

Thus *existence* becomes the key definer of God and consequently of the self. Conceiving of existence is an intellectual exercise, as Descartes will later argue, requiring nothing other than the mind. Such a conception of God and of the person in the philosophical categories of necessary and contingent existence will play a role in the ever-growing split between mind and body, a point we will return to in the discussion of Descartes in the next chapter.

Another notable work of Anselm, *Cur Deus Homo* (Why God became human), explores the question, why the incarnation? Here again we find Anselm delighting in the knowledge that human reason can come to the same conclusion that revelation provides. In that argument, Anselm proposes in syllogistic form the idea that God became human because only the one who is both divine and human can resolve the situation in which the human race found itself after the Fall of Adam and Eve. This work is also significant for the way in which it redefined classical understandings of salvation and the atonement.

For much of the first millennium, Christian theologians held to a "ransom" interpretation of the meaning of Christ's life and death on the cross. This view held that in their sin Adam and Eve had been taken captive by the devil, and God had to pay a ransom to the devil in order to save humanity. The sacrifice of Jesus paid that ransom. Anselm, however, took a different tack in his argument by placing it in the context of medieval understandings of honor-based relationships between lords and their serfs. In their sin, Anselm argued, Adam and Eve had violated the relationship of honor and trust between the Lord (God) and the servant (humanity). Such a violation upset the stability of the order of the world and had to be restored. But this restoration, while it ought to be accomplished by humanity, could not be, since it was utterly beyond human capability. While it was possible for the divine to accomplish this, Anselm believed that this was entirely inappropriate. He concluded that only the one who was both divine *and* human could do this, since for him it would be both possible *and* appropriate. This one who was both divine and human could restore the fractured relationship between God and humanity. This was (happily) accomplished by Jesus Christ, true God and true man.[6]

In medieval society all relationships had rules, and in this view Adam and Eve had violated the rules of their relationship with God. A hierarchical order of creation was assumed by medieval thinkers and, indeed, by nearly all ancient thinkers; in fact, without order, creation would be chaotic. In addition, we can note that Anselm's understanding of the sin of Adam and Eve emphasized its cosmic dimensions in upsetting the relationship between creature and creator and was a far less personal or existential conception than we see in Augustine and certainly in later figures such as Luther.

What is remarkable about Anselm's work, for our purposes here, is his method of setting aside revelation in the form of Scripture ("supposing Christ were left out of the case"[7]) and *thinking through* the logical dimensions of theology: How can we come to understand this great mystery without the assistance of the testimony of the Bible? Anselm was confident that human reason could come to the same conclusions that we learned from Scripture. And while this knowledge was made possible through God's grace, nevertheless it showed the high place in which human reason found itself.

The significance of human reason will only grow in significance in the Middle Ages and ultimately will become one of the crucial issues that

---

6. See Elizabeth Johnson's "Jesus and Salvation," *Proceedings of the Forty-Ninth Annual Convention of the Catholic Theological Society of America* (June 9–12, 1994): 1-18, on the long and successful "run" of Anselm's theory of salvation.

7. Anselm, *Cur Deus Homo*, 261.

divide Catholics and Protestants. Within a short period of time, theology itself will move from a primarily monastic location to the university, and this transition continues to be a controversial one even in the present. Does a theologian have to be a believer? What is the role of reason in relation to faith? Anselm's confidence in the power of human reason is a particularly Catholic approach that many Protestants find unwarranted, given their emphasis on the immensity of human sinfulness.

Monasticism and Living One's Faith

I noted above Anselm's "cosmic" understanding of sin—that is, the sense that the Fall of Adam resulted in humanity's relationship with God in need of restoration. Anselm did not deal as directly with the more personal dimensions of sin. This was, however, something with which the monastic tradition from another corner of the European world did concern itself; in doing so, this tradition has also left a lasting legacy particularly for Roman Catholicism's understanding of sin and the sacrament of penance.

As Christianity spread across Europe, and especially as it spread into the lands that we now call England, Scotland, and Ireland, it developed its own unique regional characteristics, as it did everywhere it took root. Monasticism was one of the dominant religious institutions during this time, and some of the practices within the monasteries began to permeate the religious lives of the local people. Each monk had his or her own spiritual director, and the practice of confessing one's sins to one's confessor developed both in the monastery and in the surrounding lay community. The Celtic tradition developed the *anamchara*—the "spiritual friend" in Gaelic.[8] Eventually, books called "penitential manuals" were developed so as to regularize the kinds of penances imposed on sinners. These works provide a fascinating window into the moral lives and concerns of medieval Christians.[9]

Augustine's understanding of sin as a complete personal rupture of the person's integrity and relationship with God and his insistence on the importance of grace for salvation has been one of his most enduring legacies. For Augustine, none of our human acts is free from sin. We

8. For a contemporary discussion, see Kenneth Leech, *Soul Friend*, new rev. ed. (Harrisburg, PA: Morehouse Publishing Co., 2001).

9. John T. McNeill and Helena M. Garner, *Medieval Handbooks of Penance: A Translation of the Principal* libri poenitentiales *and Selections from Related Documents* (New York: Octagon Books, 1965).

inevitably inherit sin from our parents; even newborn infants are not free from the taint of original sin. Recall Augustine's condemnation of Pelagianism for its idea that sin is learned from one's environment: if, in fact, we learn sin, then we can unlearn it and through our own efforts make our way to God. The problem with this for Augustine is that one comes to rely on oneself and one's own efforts rather than on God. Thus sin surrounds us; we cannot avoid it, and only God can save us from our sin.[10]

The penitential manuals attempted to define and quantify sin, a development that was both helpful and potentially open to abuse. As a result, both monks and their lay counterparts came to see the practice of penance in more individualistic terms. Where penance had formerly been a public practice (think of the sinner wearing sackcloth and ashes and whose practice of penance would have made it clear to the community what the sin was), it now became private and individual. Also, the penances assigned to particular sins were regularized so that the normal penance for breaking a fast or for adultery, to take just two examples, were consistent.

The effect that this had on theological anthropology was that the person's self-understanding in relation to God became far more organized and even quantified. The church's definition of sinfulness became more act oriented than relationship oriented, a heritage that we still have in the present. By the time of the thirteenth century, when Thomas Aquinas's *Summa Theologiae* was written, both sin and grace were highly organized and quantified, a point to which we will return later in this chapter.

The Desire for God

The other dimension of the medieval sense of the person, à la LeClercq, is the desire for God. It is helpful for modern readers to note the centrality of the Bible for monastic culture, as it was interwoven with the daily liturgy. In his Rule,[11] Benedict laid out the formal prayers of the Divine Office, which involved reciting all of the Psalms within a

10. See, e.g., "The Spirit and the Letter," in *Answer to the Pelagians: The Works of Saint Augustine for the 21st Century*, I/23, trans. Roland J. Teske, SJ (Hyde Park, NY: New City Press, 1997).

11. *Rule of Saint Benedict 1980*, ed. Timothy Fry (Collegeville, MN: Liturgical Press, 1981).

week.[12] One of the most frequently commented-upon biblical texts during the medieval period was the Song of Songs, that most sensual and graphic biblical paean to erotic love. The many commentaries on this work suggest that one could characterize the person in the medieval period as the "lover of God."[13]

Monastic life involved singing the Divine Office eight times a day, and we owe a great deal to the monastic composers of the music for the Psalms. One of the most unique representatives of monastic culture in the Middle Ages is Hildegard of Bingen (1098–1179), whose thought on music was central to her thinking about the human relationship to God.[14] Hildegard was remarkable: she was an artist, composer, playwright, scientist, and theologian. Like most male and female thinkers of her time, she believed that women were inferior to men, although she herself is an outstanding example of their equality. She experienced mystical visions of God and the cosmos, and the pictorial representations of these visions remain stunning in their complexity and beauty.[15] She also possessed a "musical" understanding of Christology and humanity, and this musicality affected her vision of monastic life and of human beings.

For Hildegard, the human body itself was a musical instrument, and Jesus Christ was the "Song of God" "whose music restores harmony to divine-human relations."[16] Interestingly, in Hildegard's dramatic depiction of the Fall, Satan cannot sing; the Evil One is incapable of sounding the harmony that is central to the life of the Christian.[17] Toward the end of Hildegard's life, she became involved in a conflict with the local bishop, and for a time her community was under interdict and forbidden to sing the Office; they could only speak the words, not sing them. The

12. *Breviary: The Hours of the Divine Office in English and Latin*, vols. 1–3 (Collegeville, MN: Liturgical Press, 1963–64).

13. See especially Bernard of Clairvaux, *On the Song of Songs*, vols. 1–4, trans. Kilian Walsh (Spencer, MA: Cistercian Publications, 1971–80).

14. See Margot Fassler, "Composer and Dramatist: 'Melodious Singing and the Freshness of Remorse,'" in *Voice of the Living Light: Hildegard of Bingen and Her World*, ed. Barbara Newman (Berkeley: University of California Press, 1998).

15. An internet search for Hildegard of Bingen will result in many websites with these images.

16. Heidi Epstein, "Immanence and Music Incarnate: Prelude to a Feminist Theology of Music," in *The Annual Review of Women in World Religions*, vol. 5, ed. Arvind Sharma and Katherine K. Young (Albany: State University of New York Press, 1999), 98, 100.

17. See ibid., 97.

experience was devastating to her, but ultimately the interdict was lifted and the singing resumed.

Like many of the women writers of her time, Hildegard identified the humanity of Christ with women; the divinity of Christ was connected with men. To modern readers, this understanding of women is profoundly unfeminist: she saw Eve as the one who brought humanity to its downfall and women as possessing a weaker will than men. Yet, as Caroline Walker Bynum points out, while many medieval women writers saw women as inferior to men and as responsible for the Fall, they also saw women and women's humanity as central in the work of salvation, in that it was only through God taking on flesh in Christ that humanity was saved. As Bynum points out, "The image of both sinful *and saved* humanity is the image of women."[18]

The desire of humans for God overflows in the medieval period, as holy men and women pour out their love for God in commentaries on the Song of Songs (Bernard of Clairvaux's being one of the best known) and in spiritual writings that portray the soul in a relationship of love with its spouse, God. The spousal metaphor for the relationship between human and divine is an ancient one, preceding even the Hebrew Scriptures in the erotic love poetry of ancient Mediterranean religion. It was later developed in the prophetic literature, in Paul, and in the early church. As we will see later in this volume, this metaphor is not without significant problems in the present, particularly with regard to conceptions of gender, where men always take the place of God as bridegroom and women the place of humanity as bride. Yet these depictions of the relationship between God and the human in the language of bridegroom and bride speak to the hunger of the human heart for God.

Another somewhat later significant thinker—she lived as an anchoress, a holy person attached ("anchored") to a church—is Julian of Norwich (1342 to ca. 1416). Julian too experienced mystical visions and, like other women mystics of the time, was encouraged to write a record of them.[19] Julian is important for her "alternative" understanding of sin. Unlike the understandings of Augustine and Anselm, where humanity's desires set the stage for its downfall, Julian's understanding of the Fall was much softer, so to speak, on the human than were her male

---

18. Caroline Walker Bynum, *Holy Feast and Holy Fast: The Religious Significance of Food to Medieval Women* (Berkeley: University of California Press, 1987), 265.

19. Julian of Norwich, *Revelations of Divine Love*, trans. Elizabeth Spearing (New York: Penguin Group, 1998).

counterparts. In Julian's vision, an eager servant rushes out to do the Lord's business, but in his eagerness he falls into a ditch and cannot get out. The Lord looks upon him with sadness and kindness.[20] Such a vision of human sinfulness sees it less as a deliberate turning away from God and more as a desperately sad situation in which we all find ourselves.

Scholasticism and Thomas Aquinas

Thomas Aquinas's (ca. 1225–74) understanding of the human person in relation to self, God, and other persons remains powerfully influential into the present. Unlike so many of his theological predecessors who were sons and daughters of the Platonic tradition, Thomas relied on a philosopher whose writings had recently been (re)discovered by Muslim and Jewish scholars and whose ideas marked a distinctly different approach to the human and to the world at large.

Aristotle—referred to by Thomas in much of his writing simply as "The Philosopher"—was a biologist by training and remained always attentive to his physical surroundings. Unlike Plato and the idealist tradition that followed his thought, Aristotle was an empiricist who took his guidance from observation of the world around him. And while the Platonist Augustine was still the most frequently cited writer in Thomas's works, the heritage of Aristotle was key.

The various dimensions of Thomas's understanding of the person occupy much of his most famous work, the *Summa Theologiae*. While the first part of this work is concerned with God and God's attributes (the "source" of the Christian life), and the third part is concerned with Jesus Christ and the church (the way back to God), the second part—in two large subsections—concerns the ultimate orientation of the human being and the ways, both good and bad, that human beings live out their lives in relation to themselves, to God, and to others.

Let me give a brief outline of Thomas's understanding of the human being. First, human beings are created by God in God's image and likeness: "Man is said to be made in God's image, in so far as the image implies *an intelligent being endowed with free-will and self-movement*."[21] Our creaturely status means that we are ultimately oriented toward God as

20. I am indebted to my students for their focus on Julian, particularly Denise Starkey.

21. Thomas Aquinas, *Summa Theologiae*, trans. Fathers of the English Dominican Province (Westminster, MD: Christian Classics, 1948 [1911]), I-II, prologue to q. 1 (hereafter cited as ST). Italics in original.

our final end. Like any other created being, we have "natural ends" (or purposes), but unlike other created beings who act for ends—the "end" of a mosquito, for example, is to suck blood from other living creatures— human beings act intentionally toward their ends ("Man differs from irrational animals in this, that he is master of his actions"[22]). Our human end is happiness, Thomas argues, citing Augustine, but as humans created in God's image, our ultimate happiness will not be in the form of riches, wealth, or power but rather in the beatific vision, when we will see God. On this point, Thomas makes a comment that is especially pertinent to the theme of this book: he notes that "man is not perfectly happy, so long as something remains for him to desire and seek." [23] The restlessness mentioned by Augustine that I quoted in the epigraph to the opening chapter of this book is familiar to Thomas as well. There is a "natural" desire in human beings for knowledge, a natural "wonder" that "causes inquiry" and will not be satisfied until we are face to face with God.[24]

Second, the stress on the intellect that we saw with Anselm continues with Thomas; in the question that investigates "those things that are required for happiness,"[25] he asks "whether the body is necessary for man's happiness"[26] and concludes that, ultimately, it is not. In a telling comment that modern neuroscientists would dispute, Thomas writes, "For the intellect needs not the body, for its operation, save on account of the phantasms, wherein it looks on the intelligible truth."[27] Yet Thomas does not easily dismiss the importance of the body, noting that it is "necessary for the happiness of this life," and in a very interesting way Thomas observes that there is a close relationship between soul and body that will only be made perfect in the final resurrection:

> For the soul desires to enjoy God in such a way that the enjoyment also may overflow into the body, as far as possible. And therefore, as long as it enjoys God, without the fellowship of the body, its appetite is at rest in that which it has, in such a way, that it would still wish the body to attain to its share.[28]

22. Ibid., I-II, q. 1.
23. Ibid., I-II, q. 1, a. 8.
24. Later on, we will see how Karl Rahner argues that even in this "face-to-face" vision of God, God will still remain Ultimate Mystery to us; this shows God's utter incomprehensibility.
25. ST I-II, q. 4.
26. Ibid., I-II, q. 4, a. 5.
27. Ibid.
28. Ibid., I-II, q. 4, a. 5, ad. 4.

This poignant comment about the soul's wistful hope for the body's complete happiness is a testimony to the significance of the body in a tradition that holds the incarnation as central.

To sum up, Thomas's anthropology sees the world, and more specifically the human, in two related ways. First, there is the perspective that understands the so-called natural processes of biological and human life as part of the natural law.[29] As I noted above, all creatures have a natural end that is intended by God and is part of our makeup. But, second, the added perspective is that of grace. In the Fall our human nature "lost" its supernatural powers, and even its natural powers were diminished. But in Christ we have been restored to grace. Yet as Karl Rahner will note in the twentieth century, the idea of "pure nature" in Thomas is really a "remainder concept," an abstraction, in that all of creation is "always, already" graced by God as *created* and as *redeemed*.[30]

Thomas's understanding of grace is significant in a number of ways. First, it develops the relationship between our "natural" existence and our existence as related to God. As the famous saying goes, "Grace perfects nature; it does not destroy it."[31] That is to say, the integrity of created reality is respected; God's grace works on and with creation to bring it to its fulfillment.[32] Human nature is "not altogether corrupted by sin . . . [and] it can, by virtue of its natural endowments, work some particular good."[33] It cannot, however, attain to its ultimate end, happiness with God, without God's grace. Second, Thomas's understanding of grace, in correspondence with his understanding of sin, spells out and parses the ways that grace works within the person. Careful thinker that he is, Thomas sorts out the various ways that grace can be understood (sanctifying and gratuitous, operating and cooperating, prevenient and subsequent) and considers the sticky question of merit—that is, whether human beings can ever "deserve" grace. While none of us could ever "earn" grace, it is possible, technically, to "merit" an increase of grace through good actions, although grace itself is entirely unmerited and

29. For a masterful treatment, see Jean Porter, *Nature as Reason: A Thomistic Theory of the Natural Law* (Grand Rapids, MI: Eerdmans, 2005).

30. See Karl Rahner, "Concerning the Relationship of Nature and Grace," in *Theological Investigations*, vol. 1, and "Nature and Grace," in *Theological Investigations*, vol. 4 (Baltimore, MD: Helicon Press, 1961, 1999).

31. ST I, q. 1, a. 9, ad. 2.

32. Ibid., I-II, q. 109.

33. Ibid., I-II, q. 109, a. 2.

comes to us only from God's generous love. The issue of grace will be one of the most contentious issues in the Reformation.

For Thomas, human life is a process of journeying toward God, our ultimate end and source of eternal happiness. Furthermore, since the "natural" has its own integrity and significance, there is no actual separation between natural and supernatural life, although he discusses the theoretical distinctions at length. So our human intentions and actions are all significant, both in their own right and in relation to God. Nearly all of the second part of the *Summa* takes up various dimensions of human actions and views them in light of their relationship to the persons involved and to God.

Thomas's descriptions of human virtues and vices are sometimes illuminating (see his discussion of the virtue of prudence[34]), sometimes puzzling (why one should love one's father more than one's mother[35]), and sometimes downright appalling (why masturbation is a greater evil than rape[36]). His discussion of the creation of woman as a "misbegotten male"[37] is one that is often cited as an example of the misogyny of the Christian tradition. Yet, feminist that I am, I would still argue that Thomas was working on the basis of the best scientific evidence that he had available within the intellectual and social context and confines of his time. Were he alive today, he would, I am sure, be obliged to argue that we are all biologically actually "first-begotten females." Whether he could escape the other attributes of an all-male clerical hierarchy is another question altogether.

The scholastic understanding of the person, as seen in Thomas, is a balanced one involving natural and supernatural in a clearly ordered universe where everyone has his or her place (God, angels, men, women, animals, in descending order) and where our "natural" experiences provide the guidelines for living a Christian moral life. This picture of existence will not last long as the intellectual and social movements of the ensuing centuries will come to challenge this image.

The Reformation

The two and a half centuries between Thomas Aquinas and the Reformation mark a period of enormous social, political, and intellectual

34. Ibid., II-II, qq. 47–50.
35. Ibid., II-II, q. 26, a. 11.
36. Ibid., II-II, q. 154, a. 12.
37. Ibid., I, q. 93.

turmoil and change. The synthesis of the late medieval period came apart as philosophers and theologians debated in mind-boggling complexity the capacity of human thought and the powers of the will. Also, the Black Death of the fourteenth century devastated the population of Europe, and new movements of lay people and a changing economy began to challenge the stable hierarchical order of the high Middle Ages. The invention of the printing press in the mid-fifteenth century, seemingly a technical innovation far removed from theology, would have a powerful impact on theologies of the person in the years to come.[38]

Martin Luther

In 1517, as the story goes, an Augustinian monk named Martin Luther (1485–1546) posted his ninety-five theses on a church door in Wittenberg, Germany. Such a gesture was not unusual in a university town: this was basically an invitation to a debate. But behind Luther's action was an increasing concern and dismay with the way that human salvation was understood in the Roman Catholic Church. Along with the quantification of sin and grace that has been mentioned above was a system of "indulgences," technically a share in the overflowing merit earned for humanity by Christ but increasingly practiced as a way to raise money while preying on the worries of Christians over their own fate in the life to come and those of their dearly departed.

Luther's own experiences were central to his theology. As a young monk, he constantly worried about the state of his soul, since he felt that he could never remain free of sin. No matter how great his efforts, he still sinned. But in reading the letters of St. Paul, he came to a fateful realization: we are free of the law and can rely on Christ who has saved us. This experience was ultimately summed up in one of Luther's famous dialectical sayings: *simul justus et peccator*—that is, we are at the same time both justified and sinners. No amount of effort on our part, and certainly no pile of money to buy our way out of purgatory into heaven, would have any effect on our salvation. This recognition of the saving knowledge from the Scriptures led Luther to another conclusion: *sola fide, sola gratia, sola scriptura*—faith alone, grace alone, Scripture alone. That is, we are not to rely upon the church, the clergy, rational knowledge, or ourselves: we are to rely upon God alone, as we find God in the Scriptures.

---

38. See Charles Taylor, *A Secular Age* (Cambridge, MA: Harvard University Press, 2007), 95.

Moreover, in contrast to Thomas's ideas that we can come to a natural knowledge of God through our own reason (cf. the "five ways" of understanding the existence of God[39] and how grace does not destroy but perfects nature) and that our "natural" inclinations form the basis of our moral lives, Luther argued that the human will is utterly bound to sin and can only be saved by reliance on Christ. Scripture is the only reliable source of knowledge—Luther would have some choice and colorful words for academic theology—and the human person should consider himself or herself as a cesspool of evil before God.

Luther's theology is "dialectical"; that is, he tends to put opposite concepts in tension with each other. His is not the cool, rational, measured understanding of the person that we see in Thomas. Luther's own volatile personality comes through in much of his writing. For example, in his treatise "The Freedom of the Christian," Luther provides us with another memorable formula: "A Christian is a perfectly free lord of all, subject to none. A Christian is a perfectly dutiful servant of all, subject to all."[40] On the one hand, in Christ we are free from the law; works have nothing to do with our status before God and are even dangerous because we tend to rely on them for our self-justification. Yet on the other hand, insofar as we are servants of all, good works will inevitably flow from our faith: "Good works do not make a good man, but a good man does good works."[41]

Unlike Thomas, Luther does not believe that our basic human nature is good; rather, we ought to despair of ourselves and our own sinfulness. This despair drives us to Christ, where we "put on Christ" so that God sees not our sinfulness but only Christ. Our will is *not* free, he argues against Erasmus. This theological anthropology is a strikingly different one than that of Thomas and the scholastics.

Yet Luther's theology, while in a sense rejecting reliance upon the self, was, in fact, the culmination of a way of thinking that had been slowly developing in the church from the Middle Ages and beyond. Rather than seeing oneself as part of a "great chain of being," the human person was now an individual who could gain saving knowledge by reading the Scriptures on one's own and not only through the church. The Word was central to Luther's message, and while he did have a

---

39. ST I, q. 2, a. 3.
40. Martin Luther, "Freedom of a Christian," in *Martin Luther: Selections from His Writings*, ed. John Dillenberger (New York: Anchor Books, 1961), 53.
41. Ibid., 69.

sacramental theology, still the sacraments were the promise of God made concrete. The development of the modern individual self has strong roots in the Reformation.[42]

Luther followed much of Augustine's thought on the inherent sinfulness of the human person, and his dialectical understanding of the person is an example of what David Tracy calls the Protestant "dialectical imagination."[43] Whereas the Catholic tradition tends to operate with an "analogical imagination"—seeing the traces of God in nature, where grace builds on and perfects nature, where our "natural" orientation is the basis of virtuous acts—the dialectical imagination sees God and human in contrast, so that our despair is the flip side of our absolute trust in God, where the depth of our sinfulness is the flip side of the immensity of God's grace, and where our human knowledge is useless in relation to the Scriptures in knowing God. It can be argued that both perspectives are necessary for a full appreciation of the riches of the tradition. The Catholic analogical imagination can use the corrective of the Protestant sense of sin, especially when one forgets its devastating effects; the Protestant dialectical imagination can also use the corrective of the Catholic appreciation of the beauty of the world. Particularly for theological anthropology, both a Protestant awareness of human sinfulness and a Catholic sense of the human capacity for good are necessary for an adequate understanding of the person.

John Calvin

John Calvin (1509–64) is most often remembered for his doctrine of predestination and for the profound influence that Calvinist thought has had, especially in North America. In terms of his thinking on the person, Calvin follows Luther in maintaining a strong sense of human sinfulness, particularly in opposition to Roman Catholic understandings of sin and grace. While later Calvinist thinkers will characterize Calvinist thought as seeing human beings as "totally depraved" (cf. the Synod of Dort in 1619), Calvin did hold that there was a "spark" of divinity in humanity despite our sin: "God himself has implanted in all men a certain under-

---

42. See Charles Taylor, *Sources of the Self* (Cambridge, MA: Harvard University Press, 1989), 211–302.

43. David Tracy, *The Analogical Imagination: Christian Theology and the Culture of Pluralism* (New York: Crossroad, 1982), 414–21.

standing of his divine majesty."[44] This sense, Calvin argues a few pages later in the *Institutes*, his massive and systematic treatment of everything related to the Christian religion, "can never be effaced," but human beings "are puffed up and swollen with all the more pride."[45] Later in the *Institutes*, in speaking about the effects of original sin, Calvin again refers to the human propensity for "deluded self-admiration": "God's truth . . . will strip us of all confidence in our own ability, deprive us of all occasion for boasting, and lead us to submission."[46] Like Luther, he was also suspicious of rational knowledge and saw the intellect as leading us to vanity, further boosting unwarranted confidence in ourselves.

In a later chapter, we will return to this sense of sin as pride and overconfidence in the self and consider its implications for marginalized groups. But for the present, it is important to note Calvin's own distinct dialectic. Where Luther's dialectic is one of sin and grace, Calvin's is more one of human humility and divine majesty. Calvin's repeated emphasis on God's majesty and power, found especially in the doctrine of predestination, is a theme that runs continuously throughout the thousand pages of the *Institutes*. Even the troublesome doctrine of predestination is based in Calvin's emphasis on the utter power and glory of God, and it can be argued that in this doctrine, Calvin was only following what he read in Scripture and in Augustine.

Human pride is insidious, Calvin argues, and it even leads philosophers to maintain that we weak and sinful people still have free will. But Calvin will have nothing of this. The more we trust in ourselves, the less we trust in God; the more we know ourselves, the more we are aware of our sinfulness: "Whoever is utterly cast down and overwhelmed by the awareness of his calamity, poverty, nakedness, and disgrace has thus advanced farthest in knowledge of himself."[47] To modern ears, this stress on humility and our utter sinfulness sounds overly negative, indeed unhealthy, and does nothing for a decent sense of self-esteem. But Calvin long predates Freud or even any of our modern psychologists who will stress the importance of having a strong sense of self-esteem. Our main task, as Calvin would see it, is to recognize our sinfulness and rely on God alone. Our human desires have been warped and distorted in sin,

---

44. John Calvin, *Institutes of the Christian Religion*, vols. 1–2 (Louisville, KY: Westminster John Knox Press, 1960), bk. I, chap. III, par. 1.

45. Ibid., bk. I, chap. V, par. 4.

46. Ibid., bk. II, chap. I, par. 2.

47. Ibid., bk. II, chap. II, par. 10.

so what we think we want is in fact the worst thing we could desire. In grace, we come to see that relying on God alone is the way to salvation.

The Council of Trent

From 1545 to 1563, the Roman Catholic bishops met in twenty-five sessions to make their formal response to the Reformation. Much of the council's work was taken up with reacting to the Reformers, and in this the bishops rejected much of the Protestant theology of human nature. While both the Reformers and the Catholics were in agreement that human beings are saved by God's grace and not by their own works (see the Augsburg Confession of 1530), nevertheless certain fundamental differences remained and were accentuated in the decrees of the council. First, in terms of the effects of sin on the person: while both sides agreed that original sin had a profoundly negative effect on human nature, Catholics rejected the Protestant view of the utter corruption of the will after the Fall. Catholics maintained that while the will was greatly weakened, free will nevertheless remained. Baptism, both sides agreed, takes away human guilt, but what remains was in dispute. Protestants held that sin remains but is no longer "imputed" to us (i.e., it is still there, but we are no longer held responsible), while Catholics believed that original sin was "wiped away" by baptism but *an inclination* to sin remains. Perhaps even more significantly, the Catholic tradition held that salvation is not assured with justification; that is, the sinner can reject God's grace and, if in a state of mortal sin, can even lose sanctifying grace altogether.[48] Calvin's insistence on irresistible grace and the perseverance of the saints—which will later find its echo in evangelical Christianity's focus on whether or not one has been saved—were viewed by the Catholic tradition as placing far too great a stress on the finality of justifying grace. And where the Catholic tradition, following Thomas Aquinas, had developed a whole system of classifying grace into its various dimensions, both Luther and Calvin rejected this, particularly with regard to such ideas as "cooperating grace" by which we are moved to "work with" God in our own salvation.[49] The Reformers agreed that this is entirely beyond the power of human beings.

The Reformation debates reflect some profoundly differing views of the person. Are we basically good, although affected by sin? Or has sin

---

48. The Decrees of the Council of Trent, Session VI, Canon XXIII. See Roger Haight, *Experience and Language of Grace* (New York: Paulist Press, 1979), 105–18.

49. Calvin, *Institutes*, bk. II, chap. II, par. 6.

so dimmed the light of God in us that we can no longer even will anything good without God? Can our "natural" knowledge lead us to knowledge of God? Or does this knowledge lead only to our increased vanity? Are we able to improve ourselves, work on getting rid of bad habits, or become better people through our own efforts? Or are we helpless without God and on our own, able only to sin? Where the Catholic tradition looked on human institutions like government as a way of making concrete the common good, Protestants like Calvin tended to see these institutions as protecting human beings from themselves.[50] These are still significant questions, and over the four hundred years since the Protestant and Catholic Reformations, they have arisen over and over again in different forms and contexts.

Women in the Reformation

The Reformation offers a somewhat mixed perspective on women. On the one hand, the Protestant Reformers, in their zeal to make all human beings equal before God without a hierarchy of clergy, religious, and laity, largely did away with religious orders for women, thus depriving many women of the opportunity for education and community in a relatively self-governing community. There developed a new role—the pastor's wife—and while it had its advantages, it took centuries before women claimed an equal role in congregational leadership. As Luther and Calvin saw it, marriage was as much a vocation as vowed religious life, which was for a tiny minority of people. This profound insight helped to restore marriage as a way to grow in grace before God and with another, refuting the idea that the better way to live one's life was as a celibate.

On the other hand, Roman Catholic women found in their own Reformation a new energy for reforming religious life and for bringing education to the people. Teresa of Avila (1515–82), along with her confidant John of the Cross (1542–91), saw the need for reform in Spain and worked to make her religious community a true community of prayer. Her own mystical visions remain powerful into the present, as does her refreshing honesty in her conversations with God. Mary Ward (1585–1645), inspired by the example of the Society of Jesus (the Jesuits), sought to found a religious order for women that would work "in the world" with women and children in need. Ward's idea of a community of women

---

50. I am indebted to Tatha Wiley for this insight; she draws on Charles Curran.

not in cloister was, however, condemned by the church, and at one point she was ill and close to death but still refused to recant her vision of a religious community for women. And in the New World, Sor Juana de la Cruz (1648–95), a self-taught scholar, refused to recant her own views on the importance of women's education. She has become known as one of the greatest scholars and poets of Mexico. In the wake of the Reformation, religious communities for men and women grew and flourished. In addition, lay spirituality for all Catholics also flowered, offering everyone the opportunity to grow in prayer and devotion.

Conclusion

The medieval and Reformation periods offer us a complex picture of the human. The development of theology as a distinct discipline, growing from biblical commentary to intellectual treatise—while still relying on biblical ideas—means that theologians have come to be more and more in conversation with philosophy, and their understanding of the human person is affected by this conversation. The questions of the effects of original sin, whether or not we have free will, and how much our intelligence assists us in finding God all occupied theologians of this period. And in relation to our overarching theme—that of human desire—these questions touch on both its positive and negative dimensions. Do we hunger for greater knowledge of God? Or do our "natural" desires push us to self-aggrandizement? These questions will take on new meaning as we move into the Enlightenment and modern periods.

Chapter Three

Resources from Modernity

Between the Reformation and the late twentieth century lie four hundred or so years of complex history in relation to thinking about the human. Consider some notable events during this time period. The Atlantic slave trade was both developed and ultimately ended, at least legally, in most of the developed world, although its long and ugly heritage lives on in the present. Scientific discoveries challenged the ways that humans viewed both their own world and the heavens above it. Political and philosophical movements of independence and liberation, from the French and American revolutions of the late eighteenth century to the independence of former European colonies in much of the global South in the mid-twentieth century, marked new ways of understanding humanity's relationship to the state and to God. It is impossible to do full justice to this complex time in this short volume. My efforts, then, will be to suggest how the Enlightenment and its heritage have affected theological understandings of human desires. The themes of this chapter will be the *desire for knowledge*, as we see it in the Scientific Revolution of the seventeenth century, in the Enlightenment, and in philosophical movements of the time, and the *desire for freedom*, as we see it in both philosophical and political movements, as well as in movements of liberation in the twentieth century. In concluding this first part, I will suggest what we can take from this survey of the tradition into contemporary reflections on theological anthropology.

It is worth noting at this point that specifically *theological* reflections on human nature took something of a back seat during the modern period. The ideas of modernity have not, for the most part, been friendly to religion, and religion has mostly responded in kind. But it would be a mistake to ignore these ideas and trends as irrelevant to a theological anthropology that claims to have any meaning in the twenty-first century.

The Desire for Knowledge

What can we really know? This question was a compelling one for the philosophers, theologians, and scientists of what I will broadly call the modern period: roughly from the time of the Reformation (early to mid-sixteenth century) until the mid-twentieth century. While Thomas Aquinas gave credit to our "natural" capacity for knowledge in the thirteenth century, by the time of the Reformation, as we saw in the previous chapter, confidence in human knowledge came to be viewed suspiciously, especially by Protestant reformers. All knowledge worth having is from God, and, as the Calvinist Synod of Dort (1619) put it, human beings are "totally depraved"; any knowledge we have on our own is woefully inadequate.[1] Nevertheless, as more and more scientific investigations and discoveries were made after the Protestant and Catholic Reformations in the sixteenth century, traditional theological conceptions of human knowledge were increasingly challenged. Authoritative sources were shifting from an external location (the church, the Bible) to an internal location: the self was now the authoritative center of knowledge.

Galileo (1564–1642) is often cited as one of the most influential figures responsible for changing the way human beings viewed themselves in relation to the universe; indeed, none other than the physicist Stephen Hawking has credited Galileo with helping to establish the foundations of modern science. Through his use of the newly developed telescope, Galileo came to the conclusion that the geocentric (earth-centered) idea of the cosmos was scientifically false and argued in favor of Copernicus's theory that the sun was in fact the center of the solar system. And since

---

1. For a succinct treatment of the Synod of Dort and its decisions, see Justo L. Gonález, *A History of Christian Thought*, rev. ed., vol. 3, *From the Protestant Reformation to the Twentieth Century* (Nashville, TN: Abingdon Press, 1975), 283–87. This synod is cited by the acronym TULIP, which summarizes the basic tenets of Calvinism: T = total depravity, U = unconditional election, L = limited atonement, I = irresistible grace, P = perseverance of the saints.

the fate of Galileo has made the Catholic Church a popular "whipping boy" for its role in coercing Galileo to recant, it is no surprise that Galileo serves as a hero for those arguing for the mutual independence of science and religion, if not the superiority of science over religion altogether.

Why was Galileo's view so controversial? For one thing, it challenged the validity of divine revelation as the source of our knowledge of the universe, and it showed that the biblical accounts were faulty, at least from a scientific perspective. More than 350 years after Galileo's death, biblical literalists still argue for the correctness of the Bible's view of the universe and its dating of the creation of the world in terms of thousands rather than millions of years, in the face of overwhelming scientific evidence to the contrary.[2] The relationship between science and religion, as we will see in a later chapter, is still a subject of much debate, but the scientific discoveries of this period forever altered the way that human beings understood their capacity for knowledge. Other significant discoveries, such as Vesalius's (1514–64) work on human anatomy, Tycho Brahe's (1546–1602) work on the elliptical orbits of the planets around the sun, and, most significantly for our purposes, René Descartes's (1596–1650) development of the scientific method, produced a profound shift in the way humans came to see their own capacity for knowledge and their place in the universe.

Descartes

Descartes is significant for theological anthropology in a number of ways. First, he developed a process for thinking, called metaphysical doubt, that located knowledge within the person alone and also solely (as he thought) within the mental capacities of the person; that is, we come to know that we know through *thinking*, not from observation, not from sense experience, and not from received or innate ideas. Descartes came to his now-famous conclusion of *cogito, ergo sum* (I think, therefore I am) by realizing that everything he encountered was subject to doubt, except for the very process of thinking itself.[3] Once he realized that the

---

2. See Galileo Galilei, "Letter to Madame Christina of Lorraine, Grand Duchess of Tuscany: Concerning the Use of Biblical Quotations in the Matter of Science" (1615), in *Discoveries and Opinions of Galileo*, trans. Stillman Drake (New York: Doubleday Anchor Books, 1957).

3. René Descartes, "Discourse on Method," in *Discourse on Method and Meditations*, trans. Laurence J. Lafleur (Upper Saddle River, NJ: Prentice Hall, 1952), 3–57.

one thing he could not doubt was his very act of doubting, he could be assured that he existed.

Second, while remaining a Catholic (although his works were later placed on the Index of Forbidden Books), Descartes established a basis for scientific method, a process in which the observer draws conclusions based on evidence. His process of sorting out a problem into its component parts and relying only on verifiable evidence still forms the basis for scientific experimentation. And when we come to know by our own process of thinking, we find the source of our authority within ourselves, not from any external source. If everything else, according to Descartes, can be doubted and our own thoughts are the only reliable source of authority, then this Copernican Revolution of the mind, this decentering of previous ways of knowing, takes place not only in the external universe but also within the person. In addition, when the mind, and not the senses, is seen as the source of our knowledge, we separate the mind from the body. What results is "Cartesian dualism," where the most important dimension of the person is the mind, and the body is utterly secondary, if not insignificant, for what we need to know.

The mind-body split will be the subject of later discussion, and it has come under attack, often for good reason, for its tendency to denigrate the body as inferior to the mind and for its relegation of those perceived to be "more embodied" (women, children, slaves) to an inferior position. But at this point it is worth making a brief comment in defense of Descartes, in light of his context. As Margaret Miles has observed, for Descartes the process of thinking does not require wealth or education or any kind of status; it requires only the time and patience needed to think—although, it must be noted, that having this time to think in itself requires certain material conditions![4] In principle, although perhaps not always in fact, favoring the mind is, at least in theory, more democratic than basing knowledge on one's sources of external knowledge, and it is inclusive of anyone's ability to think, no matter their circumstances.

Descartes had a passionate desire to know, particularly to know with certainty, and to develop a method that would advance knowledge, not merely confirm what was already known. Commentators describe Descartes's quest as one for "an order of discovery," not merely of confir-

---

4. Margaret Miles, *The Word Made Flesh: History of Christian Thought* (Malden, MA: Blackwell Publishing, 2005), 332.

mation.[5] Descartes's method has had a profound influence on both philosophy and the sciences, and certainly in relation to theological anthropology. His focus on the mind, his conviction that we can know with certainty, and his certitude that we can develop a way of thinking that is universally true have left a deep mark on how we conceive of ourselves. In postmodern retrospect, one can see how Descartes's ideas provide the foundation for what will come to be known as the "hegemonic metanarrative" of the Enlightenment: that the Western mode of thought, based on the ideas of the free, white male, determines reality for the rest of the world.[6] But that is still to come.

Hume and Kant

David Hume (1711–76) and Immanuel Kant (1724–1804) are two of the most significant philosophers of the European Enlightenment, that period of time characterized by both scientific and philosophical innovation. Their thought has also left indelible marks on both philosophical and theological conceptions of the human being, particularly in relation to their understandings of human morality. Hume is important because his conception of the human person was basically psychological. He thought that our beliefs and passions dominated our lives. He was highly skeptical of religious belief, and in his essay on miracles he thoroughly debunked religion's reliance on events that purported to go beyond the laws of nature.[7] Our beliefs largely come from reliance on others, and having real certainty is rare.

Hume argued that our religious beliefs arise out of our passions, and in this he anticipates Marx and Freud. He also suggests that religion does not help people to be more moral at all and that religion is largely superstition. In his magisterial study *Sources of the Self*, Charles Taylor writes that Hume's aim was to "anatomize the moral sentiments, in all their ultimate metaphysical arbitrariness, could-have-been-otherwiseness, in order to accept them, endorse them, know what address we are living at. Even the disengagement serves the end of an

5. See James Collins, *God in Modern Philosophy* (Chicago: H. Regnery Co., 1959), 56–64.

6. In chap. 4, I will discuss postmodernity in greater detail. A "metanarrative" is the phrase used by postmodern theorists to describe the kind of "sweeping" narrative that is at the basis of Western thought, with the (white, powerful, male) self at the center. It is "hegemonic" because of its dominant role.

7. David Hume, "Of Miracles," in *An Enquiry Concerning Human Understanding* (1748), section X.

ultimate engagement."[8] In this, Taylor argues, Hume helps to usher in a modern self, unencumbered by religion, living soberly in the world without expecting anything more.

Immanuel Kant credits Hume with "waking him from his dogmatic slumber" and pushing him to define more precisely the ways that human beings relate to themselves and to God. For Kant, religion is basically morality; that is, considered "within the limits of reason alone," religion can, at its best, help us to be moral. It does not, though, give us any real knowledge of the world or of what lies beyond the world. Like Hume, Kant was well aware of human motivations and argued that we need the idea of a Supreme Being and Eternal Justice to guide us in the way of moral action. These ideas, however, are "postulates" of our thinking and not certainties.[9] But it is also important to note that Kant was highly suspicious of any personal motivation for moral action. His ethics is "deontological," meaning that it is an ethics of *duty*, not of a final end, as we see in Thomas Aquinas's understanding of eternal happiness; nor is it an ethics of command, as we see in Calvin's conception of the significance of God's Word and our obligation to follow God's commands.[10] Rather, we do the good *because it is the good*, and any other reason undermines the genuineness and worth of each moral act. Kant's "categorical imperative," which states that any action we consider undertaking should be potentially a universal law, puts morality firmly under the rule of reason.

The Enlightenment desire for knowledge is a desire as well for certainty—for knowledge that can stand on its own, requiring no religious authority to back it up. Scientific knowledge especially comes to have a status that no other knowledge has: it can be verified or seen or demonstrated. Religion's knowledge, viewed by some Enlightenment thinkers as pure myth, based as it is on biblical stories that have little grounding in fact, is thus exposed as no knowledge at all, and the rational man (I use the masculine deliberately here) will of course choose the scientific.[11]

8. Charles Taylor, *Sources of the Self* (Cambridge, MA: Harvard University Press, 1989), 344–45.

9. See Immanuel Kant, *Critique of Practical Reason*, trans. Paul Guyer and Allen W. Wood (New York: Cambridge University Press, 1998).

10. See Immanuel Kant, *Religion within the Limits of Reason Alone*, trans. Theodore Greene and Hoyt Hudson (New York: Harper & Row, 1960).

11. This time was also significant for biblical criticism, and the historicity of biblical accounts was challenged by some of the earliest historical-critical scholars. See Albert Schweitzer, *The Quest for the Historical Jesus: A Critical Study of Its Progress from Reimarus to Wrede* (New York: Macmillan, 1964).

I should note that at this point in time, critical biblical scholarship was in its infancy. Although efforts to understand the multiple levels of meaning in the Bible date back to early Christianity, a "scientific" (i.e., verifiable) understanding of truth had come to dominate all forms of knowledge, including religious knowledge.

The idea of the human being that emerges from Enlightenment thought is, then, primarily defined by rationality. In addition, the many scientific discoveries of the period, as well as the "discoveries" of other cultures in the world, led a number of thinkers to believe that human progress is constant and inevitable, especially when European culture was compared to the more "primitive" cultures that explorers encountered in their travels.[12] The great German philosopher G. W. F. Hegel defined the movement of *Geist*, Spirit, as inevitably moving historically forward in a religious development that finds its ultimate expression in Christianity. While this idea will come under strong criticism later, Hegel and others thought that all other religions had some lesser approximation of the Spirit's development and were clearly inferior to Christianity.[13]

Nineteenth-Century Developments

Yet this same movement of Enlightenment rationality came under criticism in the nineteenth century as having an impoverished understanding of what it means to be human and of religion's role in human life. Friedrich Schleiermacher (1768–1834), a German theologian and pastor, and Søren Kierkegaard (1813–55), a Danish thinker, both attacked the rationalist systems of Kant and Hegel with a counteremphasis on feeling and passion. For Schleiermacher, religion was not simply morality "dressed up," as Kant saw it, and the church was not simply the place that helped make people more moral. Rather, for Schleiermacher, religion encompassed the "feeling of absolute dependence" on God.[14] The Christian faith, and the person of Jesus Christ in particular, was where this feeling came to its culmination, particularly in the Christian church. To disregard feeling, Schleiermacher argued, was to reduce human beings to less than what they fully were. Kierkegaard found the religion of the Enlightenment to be utterly passionless, whereas real Christianity

---

12. As recently as 1971, I took a college course entitled Primitive Religion.

13. See his *Phenomenology of Spirit* (1807) and his *Lectures on the Philosophy of Religion* (1827).

14. See Friedrich Schleiermacher, *On Religion: Speeches to Its Cultured Despisers* (New York: Cambridge University Press, 1996).

required the ultimate leap of faith into the unknown. This was exemplified by Abraham's willingness to sacrifice his own son with the confidence that even as he took his son's life, God's promise would still be kept. Kierkegaard writes of Abraham: "All that time he believed—he believed that God would not require Isaac of him, whereas he was willing nevertheless to sacrifice him if it was required. . . . He believed by virtue of the absurd."[15]

One of the greatest exemplars of the desire for knowledge about the human is the nineteenth-century scientist Charles Darwin (1809–82). He is best known for his theory of evolution, that animals and human beings descended over long periods of time from common ancestors. From his travels around the world, and particularly from his observations in the Galapagos Islands, he found evidence that life on earth was not created directly and instantaneously by God but was rather part of a long and complex process of "natural selection," by which characteristics remain that contribute to survival and to reproduction.[16]

Darwin's work and its legacy continue to play a powerful role in the ways we conceive of humanity in the present. In the nineteenth century, Christian thinkers from different traditions either fought against Darwin's theories or attempted to reconcile Christian belief with them. In the antimodernist writings of the late nineteenth and early twentieth century, popes Pius IX and X and Leo XIII argued against any theory of biblical inspiration that did not consider the Bible to be authored by Moses. The real issue for Catholic thinking was whether or not Darwin's theory challenged the theological dogma that we are all created by God. Today, I should note, the Catholic Church is fully "on board" with the theory of evolution and does not find it in conflict with the belief that God created the world. But a discussion of the church's arrival at this point is still to come.[17]

The conversation between science and religion is still a crucial one today. We will explore some of the contemporary scientific issues that are raising new questions about human uniqueness in a later chapter, but at this point it is worth pausing to consider how the world of many

---

15. Søren Kierkegaard, *Fear and Trembling and The Sickness unto Death*, trans. Walter Lowrie (Princeton, NJ: Princeton University Press, 1974 [1941]), 46.

16. See Charles Darwin, *On the Origin of Species* (Washington Square, NY: New York University Press, 1988). A very helpful source on this is Tatha Wiley, *Creationism and the Conflict over Evolution* (Eugene, OR: Cascade Books, 2009).

17. See, e.g., John F. Haught, *God After Darwin: A Theology of Evolution* (Boulder, CO: Westview Press, 2000).

Christians was utterly destabilized with the theories of Darwin in the nineteenth century and how this destabilization continues into the present. An example or two might be helpful here. In the late 1970s, a video series on world religions called *The Long Search* was released and widely used in colleges and universities.[18] The films covered indigenous religions, Hinduism, Buddhism, Judaism, Islam, and Orthodoxy, and there were two films on Western Christianity. As a beginning professor, I found them helpful and used them in my introductory classes. The film on Protestantism focused on three American Protestant congregations in Indianapolis, Indiana: one African American, one "mainline" (Methodist), and one nondenominational/evangelical. The segment on the evangelical congregation included children's songs about their biblical faith, including one that I can still recall that began, "I'm no kin to a monkey, no, no, no! A monkey's no kin to me!" Fast-forward twenty years to a conversation among a group of theologians and philosophers, all professors at my institution. In reference to a book project that we were proposing that related science and Christian theologies of the person, one senior professor strongly objected to any mention of our connections to our simian relatives. "We are not animals!" he exclaimed, to the surprise of many of us. Darwin's point, of course, was not to "reduce" human beings to a lower status, but evolution still has a powerful impact on theories of the person.

The ideas of Darwin have seriously dislocated the idea of human uniqueness, and as more and more discoveries of humans in various stages of evolution are made available, the overly simple answer that God is simply a part of this process does not resolve the many questions that continue to arise over how we can understand ourselves as created by God in the face of all of this scientific evidence. Certainly, the meaning of creation in God's image needs to be reformulated for the modern person.

Still, however, rational*ism* (although not rational*ity*) was perceived to be a threat to Christian, and especially Catholic, belief. The dogmatic pronunciation in 1854 that Mary was immaculately conceived in her mother's womb and the *Syllabus of Errors* published in 1864 were both directed at ideas of the human that ruled out direct intervention by God (as in the immaculate conception) and that defined human beings in

18. *The Long Search*, vols. 1–13, produced by Peter Montagnon (New York: Ambrose Video Pub., 1977).

"rationalistic" terms.[19] While Catholicism's conviction that faith and reason cannot ultimately be in conflict was reaffirmed by the First Vatican Council, the magisterial church struggled with the implications of Darwinism until well into the twentieth century.[20]

The Desire for Freedom

In response to Reformation ideas about the bondage of the will and in continuity with earlier tradition, Catholic theology had consistently maintained the fundamental freedom of the human person, although, one might add, with little enthusiasm for women as persons. With God's grace, we cooperate with the work of salvation in our acceptance of this grace, or we refuse it or turn our back on it and reject it, even after receiving it. The philosophers of the seventeenth and eighteenth centuries had come to understand the person in the language of freedom; indeed, Immanuel Kant referred to the Enlightenment as the time when human beings emerged from their adolescence into adulthood.[21] And while Blaise Pascal, along with the Jansenist movement in the seventeenth century, held to a much more circumscribed understanding of human freedom, the human ability to "work along with God" on one's salvation remained a very important dimension of Catholic thinking on the person.

The idea of political freedom, of course, has had an immense effect on world history; consider how President George W. Bush understood his mission in the Iraq war as bringing democracy and freedom to the rest of the world, whether they wanted it or not. The human desire for freedom is one of the distinguishing marks of the modern period, and the postmodern responses of some groups who reject Western ideas of democracy are a mystery to the Western Enlightenment mind. But this conception of the human person as radically free also has many theological dimensions.

---

19. Cf. Pius IX, " 'Syllabus,' or Collection of Modern Errors" (1864), in *The Sources of Catholic Dogma*, trans. Roy J. Deferrari (St. Louis, MO: B. Herder Book Co., 1957), especially no. 80: "The Roman Pontiff can and should reconcile and adapt himself to progress, liberalism, and the modern civilization" (p. 442).

20. Cf. Pius XII's *Humani Generis* (1950), especially nos. 5, 6, and 36.

21. Immanuel Kant, "An Answer to the Question: What is Enlightenment?" in *Political Philosophy*, trans. and ed. Mary J. Gregor (New York: Cambridge University Press, 2006 [1784]), 11–22.

The nineteenth century witnessed a number of movements for political freedom, some of which were revolutionary movements that pitted nationalism against religion and continued to challenge the church's hegemony. One significant idea that arose from these movements is that humans will freely make rational choices; another is that we do not need churches or doctrinal systems to tell us what to believe. The Enlightenment ideal of the person is not only that we are free; it is also fundamentally optimistic and believes that we will choose to do the good, if only we have the education and the means to exercise our freedom. Yet this Western idea of human freedom remained circumscribed, insofar as ideas of the freedom of women, children, and slaves were incomprehensible to many Enlightenment figures.

Slaves, Women, and Personhood

Who is a person? And who defines what a person is? Those Americans familiar with their history know that slaves were legally considered three-fifths of a person in the original United States Constitution; this was only changed with the Thirteenth and Fourteenth Amendments in 1865 and 1868, respectively.[22] Biblical passages refer to slavery as a matter of course, and such passages were used in arguments against abolition in the United States in the nineteenth century.[23] The long legacy of slavery and racism has left deep scars on the face of American religion.[24] Movements for the abolition of slavery long predate the American and English abolitionist movements, and in fact slavery was condemned by a series of popes and by religious figures such as Bartolome de las Casas, who had formerly owned slaves, and as early as Thomas Aquinas, who

22. Art. I, sec. 2, par. 3 of the United States Constitution reads, "Representatives and direct Taxes shall be apportioned among the several States which may be included within this Union, according to their respective Numbers, which shall be determined by adding to the whole Number of free Persons, including those bound to Service for a Term of Year, excluding Indians not taxed, three fifths of all other Persons." The Thirteenth Amendment officially abolished slavery; however, only with the Fourteenth Amendment, par. 2, is the so-called three-fifths compromise modified: "Representatives [of the House of Representatives] shall be apportioned . . . counting the whole number of persons in each State, excluding Indians not taxed."

23. See John T. McGreevy, *Catholicism and American Freedom* (New York: W. W. Norton, 2003), chaps. 3 and 4.

24. See Bryan Massingale, *Racial Justice and the Catholic Church* (Maryknoll, NY: Orbis Books, 2010); and M. Shawn Copeland, *Enfleshing Freedom: Body, Race, and Being* (Minneapolis: Fortress Press, 2010).

deferred to the church's view.[25] Nevertheless, the slave trade that flourished between the sixteenth and nineteenth centuries was managed by men who for the most part considered themselves good Christians, and slaves were bought and sold by people who would have no hesitation in calling themselves the same. The remorse of one former slave trader was immortalized in the hymn "Amazing Grace," in which he described himself as a "wretch" who "once was lost but now am found, was blind but now I see."[26]

The movement for women's suffrage (the right to vote) was closely related to the abolitionist movement; in fact, some of the American women who were leaders in the movement for abolition became keenly aware of their own oppression only when they attended a meeting in England on abolition and were relegated to the balcony and denied the right to speak.[27] They returned to the United States and formed their own movement, declaring their rights as women to be full citizens with the right to vote.[28] Yet as these (white) women fought for this right, many of them justified their arguments on the basis of white women's alleged superiority to black men, arguing that it would be a scandal to give the vote to ignorant former slaves but not to (educated) white women. What is at stake in the issue of the full personhood of slaves and women?

---

25. For a remarkable historical analysis of the development of the church's teaching on slavery through official documents like the ones cited, see John T. Noonan, *A Church That Can and Cannot Change: The Development of Catholic Moral Teaching* (Notre Dame, IN: University of Notre Dame Press, 2005). Pope Nicholas V's papal bull *Dum Diversas* (1452) granted permission to the kingdoms of Spain and Portugal to "subjugate the Saracens and pagans and unbelievers . . . and to reduce their persons into perpetual slavery" (Noonan, 62). According to Noonan, Nicholas V gave the Portuguese king, Alfonso V, the right to do this in June 1452, and the following January he issued a bull, *Romanus Pontifex*, that spelled this out. Pope Paul III's papal bull *Sublimus Dei* (1537) forbade the enslavement of the indigenous populations of the New World; the official statement included all peoples, "that they may and should, freely and legitimately, enjoy their liberty and the possession of their property." *Papal Encyclicals Online*, http://www.papalencyclicals.net/Paul03/p3subli.htm.

26. Cf. the video recording *Amazing Grace with Bill Moyers*, produced and directed by Elena Mannes (Alexandria, VA: PBS Video, 1990).

27. Cf. Judith Wellman, *The Road to Seneca Falls: Elizabeth Cady Stanton and the First Women's Rights Convention* (Urbana, IL: University of Illinois Press, 2004), 58–64.

28. And many of these women were aghast at the fact that black men were given the right to vote before white women were. Cf. Wellman, *The Road to Seneca Falls*, 226–27.

For one thing, there has long been a hierarchical ordering of society that has its roots in ancient understandings of the cosmos (i.e., "the great chain of being") in which humans were seen as having dominion over the earth. Class and caste systems have persisted in many societies.[29] For the ancient and medieval mentality, a lack of hierarchical ordering meant chaos. The more egalitarian understanding of human beings that began to develop in the late medieval period and found its way into economics and politics more often than not assumed that this equality applied only to free, white men. Women and slaves were in need of protection at best, or, at worst, they needed to be dominated by men because of their surprisingly less rational, sometimes even savage, natures.

For a religious and philosophical tradition that defined the human by his (the masculine is deliberately used here) rational capacity, the full personhood of slaves and of women challenged the received meanings of rationality and civilization that hid privileges, interests, and power. The obvious lack of educational opportunities for slaves and for women certainly worked against their full exercise of rationality, and while there were exceptions to this rule—women or slaves were sometimes given access to education—for the most part, education was thought to be harmful to (white, Western) women's "more delicate" natures and simply out of the question for slaves, who were perceived to be closer to "savage" animal nature than white, Western men or women.

The process that has led to full legal enfranchisement for both slaves and women has been a long and difficult one, and the legacy of slavery in particular continues to haunt the United States. Normative personhood is still defined in such a way as to assume whiteness,[30] and while overt sexism has diminished in some ways, particularly in the global North,[31] violence against women continues to be epidemic in all parts of the world.

It is beyond the scope of this short book to determine the causes of racism, but it must be said that racism has long and deep roots that are probably linked to economics, social conditioning, and personal history

29. See Jim Yardley, "In India, Castes, Honor and Killings Intertwine," *New York Times*, July 9, 2010.

30. See Laurie Cassidy and Alexander Mikulich, eds., *Interrupting White Privilege* (Maryknoll, NY: Orbis Books, 2007).

31. Since the program's inception in the 1960s, white women have benefitted from affirmative action more than men and women of color. See "Reverse Discrimination Complaints Rare, Labor Study Reports," *New York Times*, March 31, 1995.

in various ways. Racism is structural; it affects all levels of society, whites as well as people of color, and the effects of racism are particularly negative on those who do not meet the "norm" of a society.[32] During the 1950s and 60s, the American civil rights movement struggled to establish the full humanity of black people and met legislative success with the Civil Rights Act of 1964. But nearly fifty years after the passage of this important legislation, racism continues to infect individuals and institutions.[33]

From a theological perspective, women's "special nature" is still assumed in papal documents. Women are defined as fundamentally maternal and relational, having a "unique" role in church and society.[34] According to official Catholic teaching, women are incapable of receiving the sacrament of ordination and therefore cannot hold any governing power in the church.[35] The Catholic Church argues for the equality of women in the secular sphere, but the sphere of the church operates under a different set of rules. And while more will be said about this in a later chapter dealing with sex and gender, it is worth noting at this point that both conscious and unconscious assumptions about gender still affect people in many ways.

32. Cf. Bryan Massingale's CTSA address, "*Vox Victimarum Vox Dei*: Malcolm X as Neglected 'Classic' for Catholic Theological Reflection," *Proceedings of the Sixty-Fifth Annual Convention of the Catholic Theological Society of America* (2010): 63–88. He recounts an experiment performed by Kiri Davis, an African American teenager, for a documentary called *A Girl Like Me*: "Using a group of twenty-one black boys and girls, the oldest of whom seem to be no more than four years old, [Ms. Davis] shows them the black doll and the white doll, identical in every way except for the color of their skins. She asks them, 'Can you show me the doll that you like best or like to play with?' The majority choose the white doll. She continues: 'Can you show me which doll is the nice doll? Can you show me the doll which looks bad?' Then she asks, 'Why is this the nice doll?' 'Because she's white.' Davis follows up: 'Why does this one look bad?' 'Because it's black.' And then the truly gut-wrenching question: 'Can you give me the doll that looks like you?' A little girl, no more than three, reaches for the white doll, visibly hesitates, and then reluctantly . . . sadly . . . pushes the interviewer the black doll. The majority of the children, 15 out of 21, preferred the white doll, and saw themselves as bearing the stigmas associated with the black one" (86).

33. In August 2010, a worker at a Hartford beer distributor shot and killed eight people, citing racism as the reason. Cf. David Owens and Dave Altimari, "9 Dead in Manchester Workplace Shooting," *The Hartford Courant*, August 3, 2010.

34. See, e.g., *Mulieris Dignitatem* (1988), *Redemptoris Mater* (1987), *Ordinatio Sacerdotalis* (1994), and *Familiaris Consortio* (1981) for different statements of Pope John Paul II regarding women and a woman's role in the church.

35. While a number of women have served as diocesan chancellors, governing power is still reserved to ordained clergy.

The "Masters of Suspicion"

Karl Marx

Paul Ricoeur's term the "Masters of Suspicion" for Marx, Nietzsche, and Freud brings these three thinkers together as united in their questioning of the free capacities of the person. In a sense, all three are perhaps the first "postmoderns" in their criticism of prevailing ideas of human freedom and rationality. Karl Marx (1818–83) was a German political philosopher who observed the workings of the growing economic system of capitalism and was dismayed at its effects on people and societies. He determined that capitalism would inevitably lead to class struggle and would ultimately be overcome in the classless society of communism. In contrast to many thinkers of his time, Marx was convinced of the communal nature of the person, though it might be said that his optimism about the possibility of a classless society reflects the general optimism about the person characteristic of the Enlightenment and the nineteenth century in general. Marx's ideas included the points that human circumstances were dependent on material reality and that human beings were producers but also able to reflect on their lives. Indeed, the process of raising the consciousness of workers who were alienated from themselves and from their work is one of Marx's signal contributions and one that was further developed by a number of later thinkers. In addition, Marx held that human reality was historical and changeable—he expected that there would be a revolution to overthrow capitalism as other systems had been overthrown in the past—and that human beings were constituted by their social relations.

Religion, Marx argued, is the "opiate of the people," a system designed by the powerful to keep the poor in their place and dependent on a vision of eternal happiness while they were taught to see their present circumstances as having little value in relation to their religious convictions.[36] Marxist theory would later be adopted by a number of liberation theologians in the twentieth century who relied on his analysis of the systems of production to argue for a political interpretation of the Gospel message. One point about Marx that is especially significant for our purposes here is his emphasis on the material conditions of human flourishing.

---

36. Karl Marx, *Introduction to a Contribution to the Critique of Hegel's Philosophy of Right*, in *Collected Works*, vol. 3 (New York: Cambridge University Press, 1976 [1843]), 3.

Much of the Catholic tradition's theological anthropology has rightly emphasized the human capacity for reason, freedom, and the desire for God. But as liberation theologians in particular have reminded us, the ability to act rationally, to live and make choices freely, and to live a life focused on the love of God is also dependent on having the necessary conditions for a decent life. The belief that what is most important in one's life is eternal life, not life as it is lived in the present, can have the result of denying the negative influence of personal and social circumstances, overlooking situations of oppression and injustice, and, in effect, valuing the mind and spirit over the body.

The question of suffering is one that is closely related to this point. To what extent is suffering to be endured, as a share in the suffering of Christ, as an inevitable dimension of human life? Many older Catholics, especially women, will recall being told to "offer up" their hurts, illnesses, and sufferings as a way to incorporate suffering into their religious life: to willingly accept suffering was a virtue, something that the saints did and that we were taught to emulate. As liberation theologians see Marx, his ideas are helpful in analyzing the sources of oppression so that circumstances that are unjust and keep people in unnecessary conditions of suffering can be identified and opposed. Christ's message, these theologians argue, did not ignore the material circumstances of people's lives; indeed, the parables of Jesus frequently refer to injustices in the everyday lives of people and suggest that any disciple of Jesus is bound to respond to these conditions. Salvation is, yes, ultimately to be fulfilled in eternity, but this does not mean that human beings are to suffer needlessly under unjust conditions. Roger Haight has observed that in some of its forms, liberation theology can be interpreted as a kind of "new Pelagianism," where we work out our salvation through our own efforts, although Haight's own evaluation of liberation theology is quite positive.[37] Marx's main concern was indeed human freedom, and while we may not agree with his idea that a classless society is possible, especially after the fall of communism in 1989, many of Marx's insights remain valuable.

Sigmund Freud

Sigmund Freud (1856–1939) is another figure whose influence remains powerful today and who is deeply significant for religion. Freud was born into a Jewish family in Vienna. Although he did not practice

---

37. See Roger Haight, *The Experience and Language of Grace* (New York: Paulist Press, 1979), chap. 8.

his faith and was a harsh critic of religion, late in life he was forced to flee to London to escape the Nazi Holocaust. Freud forever changed the way that human beings came to see themselves and challenged the prevailing Enlightenment idea that we are free and rational beings.

Through his scientific process of psychoanalysis—Freud always maintained that he was first and foremost a scientist and based his conclusions on the evidence from his practice—Freud redefined the psychological makeup of the human person. Indeed, it could be said that he revolutionized the geography of the human psyche. Rather than the ideas that human beings are pure innocents until they reach puberty, that our relationships with our parents are based in love and affection, and that our motivations are strictly rational, Freud argued to the contrary that we are in fact sexual beings from birth onward, that our relationships with our parents are fraught with sexual energy, and that our real desires are for pleasure and ultimately for death. Such a message was shocking to Freud's Victorian contemporaries, as it still is today.

Freud's distinct contribution was the idea of the unconscious—that there is a level beneath our conscious awareness that plays a significant role in our lives. We are mostly unaware of the unconscious, but it emerges in some noticeable ways, especially in dreams and in slips of the tongue—"Freudian slips." But our unconscious is also the bearer of much that is significant for the person: our desires, hopes, and energies. We can tap into our unconscious through attention to our dreams, our slips, and through the practice of psychoanalysis, where a trained analyst can help us to come to know our deeper hurts and desires.

Influenced by the significance of history, both for persons and for societies, Freud argued that human beings go through distinct developmental stages in their growth, and each of these stages has a sexual element that is intrinsic to healthy human development and must be negotiated relatively successfully. Inevitably, however, we encounter problems and difficulties, and these issues will recur in our lives in the future. In this sense, we are all "neurotic," in that human life cannot lead to perfect happiness. Psychoanalysis helps to resolve these issues so that we can move from "neurotic misery" to "common unhappiness."

Especially later in his life, Freud was fascinated by the role of religion and wrote a number of significant works on the topic.[38] In *The Future of an*

---

38. See Sigmund Freud, *Moses and Monotheism* (New York: Vintage Books, 1967 [1939]); *Totem and Taboo* (New York: W. W. Norton & Co., 1950 [1913]); and *The Future of an Illusion* (New York: W. W. Norton & Co., 1961 [1927]).

Illusion, he presented religion as historically "helping to allay the terrors of nature" and providing humanity with a Father figure that would reward us in a future life. Religion had done its job, Freud noted, in providing reasons for the terrifying and the unknown and offering some solace for the inevitable disappointments that life brings. But now, he argued, religion is obsolete. In the modern, rational age, humanity needs to realize that religion is an "infantile neurosis" that needs to be set aside as we set aside our other childish beliefs. And contrary to what many believe, Freud wrote, religion does not help us to be moral; rather, it encourages us to rely on a "higher reason" for our actions and thus leaves us in a perpetual state of childhood. In the closing pages of *The Future of an Illusion*, Freud writes, "No, our science is no illusion. But an illusion it would be to suppose that what science cannot give us, we can get elsewhere."[39]

What is it that science cannot give us? Science cannot give us the idea that everything will work out, that there is a loving Father up in the sky who sees all, who protects us, and who will reward us when we die. Rather, we have to grow up and realize that life is difficult, that true happiness is an illusion, and that developing the capacity to love and work with a minimal amount of neurotic stress is about as good a life as we can hope for.

Freud's insights into human nature have not gone unnoticed by religion. Indeed, the whole area of religion and psychology owes a great deal to Freud for pointing out how our psyches and our religious ideas work together. One might say that religion in the modern world has become thoroughly "psychologized," in the sense that developmental stages of faith and of morality have become part not only of the scholarly landscape but of everyday conversation, and that we distinguish between psychological and religious dimensions of human life, both of which are essential in understanding ourselves.[40] But the basic question Freud raised, one that had been asked a century earlier by Ludwig Feuerbach, is whether in fact our religious ideas arise out of deep psychological needs. If so, should we "outgrow" them and accept the universe as it is, as Freud and others suggest? The resurgence of a "new atheism" in the first decade of

39. Freud, *The Future of an Illusion*, 71.

40. See, e.g., Lawrence Kohlberg's *Moral Stages: A Current Formulation and a Response to Critics*, with Charles Levine and Alexander Hewer (New York: Karger, 1983); Carol Gilligan's *In A Different Voice: Psychological Theory and Women's Development* (Cambridge, MA: Harvard University Press, 1982); and James Fowler's *Stages of Faith: The Psychology of Human Development and the Quest for Meaning* (San Francisco: Harper & Row, 1981).

the twenty-first century is evidence that the idea of religion being an immature, obsessional neurosis is still widely accepted.[41]

Conclusion / Twentieth-Century Issues

The Enlightenment and modern periods witnessed the development of an understanding of the intelligent, autonomous, modern person as one who can choose to be religious or not. Western theological and philosophical narratives of anthropology have assumed that "human experience" is universally shared, that we are primarily intellectual, rational beings, and that religion offers us meaning in the midst of an unfeeling, scientific universe. The optimistic "myth of progress" that is characteristic of much of the modern period has, however, been revealed as a myth in the most common sense of the word: a commonly held belief that does not hold up to experience.

World War I put an end to many of these ideas. The "war to end all wars" ended up killing millions, leaving Europe devastated, and its punitive aftermath in Germany provided the context for the development of Nazism in the 1920s and 30s and its horrific denouement in World War II. The terrible effects of colonialism in much of the global South continue to reverberate into the present, as former colonies have developed their own political and economic systems, many of which continue to struggle to survive amid economic inequities of global financial systems and other challenges.

The "modern" Enlightenment understanding of the person, while under tremendous criticism in the present—some of which we will examine in the next chapter—is still a powerful force, and it continues to challenge theological anthropology. How does Christian theology take into account the genuine contributions of the sciences, political movements for independence, forces of economic development, and challenges to traditional ideas of gender? In the following four chapters, I will take up some of these challenges and ask how a Christian understanding of the human person can be informed by the knowledge that the modern period has gained while still learning from its long tradition and being faithful to the Gospel message.

---

41. Cf. the work of the "new atheists"—e.g., Sam Harris, *The End of Faith: Religion, Terror, and the Future of Reason* (New York: W.W. Norton & Co., 2004); Richard Dawkins, *The God Delusion* (Boston: Houghton Mifflin Co., 2006); and Christopher Hitchens, *God is Not Great: How Religion Poisons Everything* (New York: Twelve, 2007).

Chapter Four

Christian Selfhood and Postmodernity

As we saw in the last chapter, the Enlightenment and modern periods developed a picture of the human being as a free, autonomous individual who faced unlimited opportunities. The modern person, to borrow the words of Voltaire's *Candide*, lived "in this best of all possible worlds."[1] Religious identity was no longer central to this modern, enlightened human being, who was finally free of the intellectual and social bonds that kept him (I use the masculine pronoun deliberately) tied to superstition. Tom Wolfe's characterization of the scions of the financial industry in the 1980s also comes to mind: "Masters of the Universe."[2] The modern "masters of the universe" could know the world and themselves through their access to scientific knowledge, which was increasing in scope on a daily basis. They could control the world through this knowledge and explore not only the world around them but also the depths of the oceans and the vastness of space. Their ability to define the world in clear terms— as a space for potentially unlimited economic growth, as following a clear historical path—has led later postmodern scholars to define this tendency as developing so-called metanarratives that purported to be universally true.[3] "Modern man" had a stable sexual, personal, familial, religious, and national identity that was clearly evident and unquestioned.

1. Voltaire, *Candide, Zadig and Selected Stories* (New York: Penguin Putnam Inc., 1981), 16.
2. Tom Wolfe, *Bonfire of the Vanities* (New York: Farrar, Straus, Giroux, 1987), 9.
3. See Michel Foucault, *The Birth of the Clinic: An Archeology of Medical Perception* (New York: Vintage Books, 1975); and Jean-François Lyotard, *The Postmodern Condition: A Report on Knowledge* (Minneapolis: University of Minnesota Press, 1993).

Of course, in reality this picture applied to a very limited number of people with substantial intellectual, social, economic, and political power, most of them in Europe and North America. Most people in the world had little education, lived under oppressive political regimes, struggled on a daily basis for the basic necessities of life, and gave little thought to the kinds of issues entertained by these "masters of the universe," as Voltaire suggested in his play. Some of the cracks in this identity were already evident in the nineteenth century, hinted at by Karl Marx and Sigmund Freud. Freud challenged the idea that we truly know ourselves, that we are what we appear to be. For Freud, one's own history, particularly one's childhood, has a profound effect on the way that one's life comes to be shaped and understood, often in ways that we only dimly understand, if we consider them at all. Marx suggested that those on the underside of society were in the shadow of a "false consciousness" that failed to recognize the unjust realities under which they lived. Movements for the abolition of slavery and for women's suffrage challenged the idea of what it meant to be a person and thus forced constitutional changes, at least in the United States and other societies in the global North. By the late twentieth century, challenges to "modern" identity were increasingly clear. The wars and genocides of the twentieth century have certainly raised the question of the morality of the "best of all possible worlds," an issue that will be explored in chapter 6. The movements of political liberation in the mid and late twentieth century made serious challenges to the power of Western hegemony (power and dominance). So the "modern" picture of the person was increasingly revealed as neither adequate nor true. Thus, the term "postmodern" has emerged as a way to name the conditions of the late twentieth and early twenty-first centuries.

"Postmodernity" is a slippery term; defining its precise meaning is impossible, since it encompasses a variety of different characterizations of a complex reality and not all scholars agree on all of its characteristics. Postmodernity is "after" (post) the modern world, but it still continues to exhibit some of the qualities of the modern world; indeed, one of the questions regarding postmodernity is whether or not it is a "correction" of modernity or an entirely new chapter of time altogether. There is ample literature on the subject that attempts to shed light on the characteristics of postmodernity, and I urge the interested reader to explore these more fully.[4] My efforts in this chapter are to try to sort through some of the

---

4. See Paul Lakeland, *Postmodernity: Christian Identity in a Fragmented Age* (Minneapolis, MN: Fortress Press, 1997). Also see Thomas Guarino, *Vattimo and Theology*

ways that this "movement," for lack of a better term, has forced theology to rethink its theological anthropology. Whether postmodernity is a friend to theology is much debated, but the issues it raises about personhood and God are significant ones indeed and worthy of consideration on our part.

Characteristics of Postmodern Selfhood

If the challenges of postmodernity have had any particular focus, it is in ideas of the self. Descartes's conception of the self-contained ego has served as the quintessential representation of the modern self: enclosed within itself, abstracted from the body, without any need to consider the social or historical conditions that bring a self to awareness. Although it is important to note the ways that Descartes's conception of the self may have some merit, particularly in its own context, its "universal" mind, in complete control of its thinking and its surroundings, has come under massive critique by postmodern thinkers. What, then, are some characteristics of postmodern selfhood, and how do these ideas critique and potentially even contribute to Christian conceptions of the person?

Fragmentation and Plurality

Let us consider the issues relating to personhood in the contemporary world. What are some of the ways that a person might understand himself or herself in relation to sexuality, family, religion, nation, or environment? The terms "fragmentation" and "plurality" are often used in relation to postmodern ideas of the self and to the contemporary situation. The fragmented self is not whole and complete but rather has potentially multiple identities, as well as a sexuality that is not simply a given but also constructed. Consider, for example, the transgender man who is biologically female but identifies as a male. One's family is not only one's biological kin group but also those with whom one has decided to affiliate and form a new kind of family, such as the same-sex male couple who contracts to have a child through a woman acquaintance. One's religion is chosen from among the many possibilities available: both within a tradition (the "cafeteria Catholic") and from among

(London: Continuum, 2009); and *The Cambridge Companion to Postmodern Theology*, ed. Kevin J. Vanhoozer (Cambridge and New York: Cambridge University Press, 2003).

different traditions (the student who considers herself a Catholic but also believes in reincarnation). One's nation is not simply where one was born but also may include the country to which one has immigrated, so that one's national loyalties may encompass more than one nation. One's environment is not only the particular location of one's own residence; it also includes other environments, as the effects of climate change are increasingly felt worldwide. Human identities are multiple and in flux.

Some of these examples may seem remote from ordinary experience (the transgender man, perhaps), but in fact most of us encounter elements of these fragmented selves daily and participate in this fragmentation ourselves. Our identities are not only the faces we present to the public in our daily lives but also all of our other identities: our Facebook page, our "avatars" on the computer games we play, our memberships in different groups. From a postmodern perspective, our sexual and gender identities are not stable and essential, as official Catholic teaching holds, but constructed, diverse, and open to ambiguity. We come to see that we are not the self-contained, individual, autonomous beings that Enlightenment philosophies suggest. We are enmeshed in different communities, relationships, identities. So our definition of what it means to be a self, a person, is no longer a seamless essential self, if it ever were so.

Social and Historical Relativity

We are all defined in ways that point to our own histories. For me, growing up in the American Midwest, being a middle child in a large Irish-Catholic family, being part of the "baby boomer" generation, being a young woman during the peak of the sexual revolution and women's liberation movements, have marked me in ways that I cannot ignore. I have become keenly aware of my own race and nationality in visits to eastern Africa, as well as of my own biases as I encounter students and colleagues whose backgrounds differ from mine. The term "social (and historical) location" has become a commonplace in identifying one's own situation, as it ought to be, although it is sometimes also used as a shorthand for avoiding fuller engagement with this relativity. Feminist and liberation theologians began to observe in the 1960s and 70s that theological understandings of the person also emerged out of a context. For example, for whom is pride, traditionally understood as the root of original sin, really a sin? For the oppressed black woman who struggles to maintain a sense of dignity in the face of everyday humiliations? Or for the "master of the universe" who controls wealth, people, and resources?

The significance of social and historical relativity means precisely that: our ideas are *related* to our contexts, and thus claims to absolute and universal truths are by definition rendered highly suspect, if not subject to dismissal altogether. While this point has many implications, perhaps the most significant are its ethical dimensions. If truth is always relative, how can one say that one thing or another is right or wrong, just or unjust? How can one criticize another person or another group on the basis of their ethical judgments? Are there truths that can transcend particular experiences, or does social and historical relativity mean that "anything goes?" The issue of relativity has many dimensions, and certainly the moral implications are some of the most profound.

The emergence of liberation theology in the late 1960s raised the issue of universal identity as some Latin American theologians, trained in Europe, returned to their home countries and came to realize that the serious issues discussed in the global North, such as the "death of God," came out of particular historical and social locations and had little if any relevance to the poor in the global South. The privileged place of the white, Western, male, advantaged (and, in theology, often celibate) view of the world—sometimes referred to by its critics as the "view from nowhere"—was toppled as voices previously unheard began to write and speak.

As I suggested above, early feminist theologians challenged the idea that original sin could be adequately defined for everyone as "pride" by pointing out how women were often socialized into roles of self-sacrifice; if anything, these theologians argued, women needed a greater sense of self-worth, not a lesser one.[5] Black theologians turned to the exodus experience for inspiration and castigated white theologians for their failure to take the liberating message of the Bible seriously.[6] Scholars from both of these perspectives argued that what had previously been seen as "reality" was in fact the view from a particular place and time. They challenged the hegemony of the previously dominant view, particularly in language and in vision.

The Linguistic Turn

While the philosopher Richard Rorty is credited with the phrase "the linguistic turn," the postmodern focus on language has been one of its

---

5. See Valerie Saiving, "Human Experience: A Feminine View," in *Womanspirit Rising: A Feminist Reader*, ed. C. P. Christ and J. Plaskow (New York: Harper, 1979).

6. See James Cone, *Black Theology of Liberation* (Philadelphia: Lippincott, 1970).

persistent themes. The "commonsense" idea is that language is something we learn to use and control by inserting our thoughts into words.[7] Language is thus seen as something we master; we speak of using language, manipulating language, and learning a new language. But the power of language is far more complex than this suggests. Thus, postmodern theorists suggest that it is language that uses us, rather than the reverse.

First, our languages predate our own awareness and consciousness. We are born into languages, and they shape the ways we think. As one theorist of postmodernity puts it, "What can be said lays down the boundaries of what can be thought."[8] Rather than our shaping language, language shapes us before we are even aware of it. Second, languages function as systems. That is, no one word can stand alone; words have significance only in relation to other words, which together form linguistic systems. Third, languages are all relative: each language bears its own cultural and historical location, and no one language defines reality in a universal sense. Those who learn another language well are familiar with the difficulty of *really* translating ideas from one culture to another.

Who we are as persons is inevitably connected with language. Some postmodern and post-Freudian thinkers such as Jacques Lacan locate selfhood in the emergence of language. Once the child is no longer primarily connected to its mother's body and can "fill in the space" that emerges in that process of individuation, the self "comes to be" in language.[9] Our personal and cultural narratives are by definition linguistic. As we construct meanings for the events of our lives, we cannot but turn to language to make sense of what is going on.

Otherness

Lorraine Bethel's 1979 challenge to white feminists, "What Chou Mean *We*, White Girl?" bluntly raises the question of who "we" are.[10] The assumed universality of the self has been powerfully challenged in recent decades, particularly by women and people of color. Bethel's

---

7. Here, Bernard Lonergan's idea of the "bias of common sense" is helpful. See his *Insight: A Study of Human Understanding* (Toronto: University of Toronto Press, 1992), 218–42.

8. Lakeland, *Postmodernity: Christian Identity in a Fragmented Age*, 19.

9. Jacques Lacan, *The Language of the Self: The Function of Language in Psychoanalysis* (Baltimore: Johns Hopkins Press, 1968).

10. See Lorraine Bethel and Barbara Smith, "What Chou Mean *We*, White Girl?" *Conditions* 5 (November 1979).

challenge was to white feminists who assumed that all women share the same experiences—not only biological but also familial and social—and thus this one particular, and privileged, group of women could speak for all women. The presumed universality of personhood—and in this case, womanhood—was revealed as partial and inclusive of the experiences of only some: for the most part, educated and privileged white women. The emergence of "other" (i.e., "other" than white, Western, straight, etc.) voices—voices from the global South, from marginalized racial, ethnic, and sexual minorities—has changed the landscape of personhood in powerful ways, and much of the political rhetoric in the United States in the first decades of the twenty-first century reflects this upheaval. The fierce debates on abortion, gay marriage, immigration, and what it means to be American—consider, for example, how Barack Obama's US citizenship and his religious identity have been questioned—all reveal that our once-stable political, religious, social, and even personal identities are no longer solid and secure. If women can decide for themselves whether or not to continue a pregnancy, if gay men and lesbians can marry, if the Americans next door speak with an accent, if an African American can be elected President of the United States, then what does it mean now, for example, to be married or to be American for the US-born, white, heterosexual male? Clearly, the repercussions of these questions are very obvious as we move through the second decade of the twenty-first century.

The assumption of the universal identity of the free white male subject could be said to characterize modern discourse on the self. This point is closely related to social and historical relativity, but what makes this point even more significant is that the "other" is no longer a distant or silent "other," but rather one whose presence is immediate and cannot be ignored. Lakeland notes that in modern "metanarratives," the "other's" voice is never heard.[11] "Man" speaks for all, and if one's thinking or experiences do not match those of the universal "man," then one is quite literally ex-centric, out on the margins, unheard. But today, the "other," be it the black woman, the formerly closeted gay man, the servant, the disabled veteran, or the "foreigner," is no longer invisible and silent; "others" are defining themselves in ways that do not match traditional norms. In the postmodern world, the "other" is oneself, or one's neighbor, or one's president. The nearness of the "other" breaks down

---

11. Lakeland, *Postmodernity: Christian Identity in a Fragmented Age*, 31.

the situation of the "modern man" as center, or "master," of the universe. There is no one center, and one wonders if there is even a self at all.

Ambiguity

Ambiguity is a quality that permeates all the characteristics of postmodernity. As I describe above, fragmentation and plurality suggest that there is more than one reality, and these realities cannot be neatly characterized or unified into one. Social and historical relativity suggest that there is no one "view from nowhere," no privileged vantage point from which one sees and judges all reality as one coherent whole. "Otherness" is an attribute not always of someone else, but sometimes of oneself and sometimes of an "other." These plural realities have to be seen in their own context, in their own languages.

The ambiguity of the postmodern situation raises numerous questions related to theological anthropology. First, ambiguity characterizes our human situation. As Ruth Page notes in her book *Ambiguity and the Presence of God*, "any human attempt at order is a logically agreed cluster of values and interpretations involving a temporary simplification of complexity and the transient arrest of some aspects of change."[12] In other words, there is no one stable cosmic order on which we pattern ourselves; rather, we invent our orders as we go along, and they are relevant for particular times and places. Especially when it comes to our ideas relating to God—and thus to ourselves as created in God's image—the idea of a Divine Being who controls the world and provides meaning to our lives can no longer have the holding power that it has had in times past. Seeing ambiguity as constitutive of our situation means that human social, political, and religious institutions can no longer claim the authority they once may have had. The "natural order" of the universe, as Page points out, is not stable and organized but rather based in change and chance.[13]

Ambiguity also has powerful ethical ramifications. If there is no one stable, centered self, if our human institutions can no longer claim divine authority, and if our languages basically reflect the particular circumstances of a given place and time, then how can we make universal moral claims? Paul Lakeland's characterization of the postmodern sensibility has quite profound moral implications: "The postmodern sensibility, let me suggest, is nonsequential, noneschatological, nonutopian, nonsystematic, nonfoundational, and, ultimately, nonpolitical. The postmodern

---

12. Ruth Page, *Ambiguity and the Presence of God* (London: SCM Press, 1985), 14.
13. Ibid., 74.

human being wants a lot but expects little. . . . Postmodernity may be tragic, but its denizens are unable to recognize tragedy."[14] The one-word comment and attitude that has permeated popular culture and the lives of many young people of the twenty-first century—"whatever"—does not suggest a firm moral foundation. And that "whatever" is indeed the conclusion of some postmodern thinkers.

Yet it is ironic, as a number of writers representing formerly "other" points of view have observed, especially minorities and women, that just as these "others" are finding their voices and claiming their own subjectivity, the "death of the subject" has been proclaimed. At this point, one is tempted to ask, the death of *which* subject? Both feminist and liberationist authors have suggested that the ambiguity of the postmodern condition is not total—that would indeed be a totalizing narrative in itself!—but rather calls for a more careful and nuanced approach to the nature of the person and to the moral life.

Christian Theological Engagement with Postmodernity

It might appear at first glance that the postmodern critique of Enlightenment and modern subjectivity is particularly hostile to religion, and this first guess would not be far off the mark. Particularly in the initial years of serious postmodern critique, religion came under heavy criticism.[15] In more recent years, however, postmodern theorists have been drawn to religion.[16] But it is nevertheless also the case that many Christian theologians have found in the postmodern critique, at the very least, a necessary corrective to some of the claims that the Christian tradition has made and, at most, a profound challenge to some of its central teachings. If we question absolute and transcendent truth, can Christianity make the claim that Jesus Christ is the absolute savior?[17] If

14. Lakeland, *Postmodernity: Christian Identity in a Fragmented Age*, 8.

15. For examples of postmodern writers who criticize religion, see the work of Richard Rorty, *Philosophy and the Mirror of Nature* (Princeton, NJ: Princeton University Press, 1980); and Judith Butler, *Gender Trouble: Feminism and the Subversion of Identity* (New York: Routledge, 2006). In recent years, however, Butler and others have turned more seriously to the consideration of religion.

16. For examples of postmodern writers who approach religion positively, see the work of Slavoj Žižek, Emmanuel Levinas, and John Caputo.

17. See, e.g., Paul Knitter, *No Other Name? A Critical Survey of Christian Attitudes toward the World Religions* (Maryknoll, NY: Orbis Books, 1985); and Roger Haight, *Jesus, Symbol of God* (Maryknoll, NY: Orbis Books, 1999).

all truth is relative, can Christians claim that their moral standards affect all human beings, not just those who call themselves Christian?[18] If we are all situated in particular ways and fragmented in our experiences, can we communicate with each other, much less claim to be subjects who make (responsible) decisions, act in relation to others, and desire a relation with God? In short, can the Christian tradition continue to make universal claims about what it means to be human?

The engagement of theologians with postmodernity is, at least in large part, a necessary task since it is the Christian theologian's responsibility to engage the tradition with the present. As we have already seen with the development of Christian understandings of the self, theologians have drawn on Platonist influences, the medieval code of honor, the thought of Aristotle, and modern ideas of historicity, in addition to their engagement with the Scriptures and the tradition of the church. In what follows I will suggest how some Christian theologians have engaged some of the critical issues of postmodernity while maintaining a commitment to what they consider to be central elements of the Christian faith.

Edward Schillebeeckx and "Anthropological Constants"

The late Flemish theologian Edward Schillebeeckx (1914–2009) was a keen observer of the world, and his theology always sought to be responsive to the temper of the times. His first work dealt with the phenomenological category of "encounter" as a way of understanding the sacraments in the modern world.[19] Sacramental theology had for centuries drawn on the ancient and medieval philosophical categories of substance and accident; Schillebeeckx's pioneering effort was to turn to more contemporary philosophical ideas, a method that continued in his later work. He turned to critical theory and contemporary biblical scholarship in an effort to draw Christian theology into further dialogue with the newest findings of modern thought and scholarship. In the second volume of his massive christological project, *Christ: The Experience of Jesus as Lord,*[20] Schillebeeckx developed a set of what he called "anthropological constants" that he argued "constitute *permanent* human impulses and

18. See John Paul II, *Veritatis Splendor*, for a critique of moral relativism.

19. Edward Schillebeeckx, *Christ the Sacrament of the Encounter with God*, trans. Paul Barrett (New York: Sheed and Ward, 1963).

20. Edward Schillebeeckx, *Christ: The Experience of Jesus as Lord*, trans. John Bowden (New York: Crossroad, 1981).

orientations, values, and spheres of value" yet at the same time cannot be specified beyond a particular time or place.[21] These constants are

1. human corporeality, nature, and the ecological environment;

2. human relationality;

3. the connection with social and institutional structures;

4. the conditioning of people by time and space;

5. the mutual relationship of theory and practice;

6. the religious and 'para-religious' consciousness of humanity; and

7. the irreducible synthesis of these seven dimensions.[22]

Schillebeeckx's purpose was to outline the dimensions of the human in the face of massive suffering, as well as to respond to views of human experience that attempt to characterize it in transcendent categories such as those of "Nature, 'ordinances of creation' and Evolution."[23] He agreed with the postmodern claim that there is no "universal human nature" and also took issue with more recent attempts to define the human in more contemporary but still "essential" ways, such as structuralism or existentialism. Although in his earlier work he relied more heavily on a phenomenological interpretation of Thomism, by the latter part of his career, he was much more aware of the contributions of critical theory and the obligation to respond to human needs in a time of unspeakable evil.

Like many postmodern thinkers, Schillebeeckx stressed the narrative and linguistic quality of human experience, which, he argued, was the place where human beings find God. But we find God not in any direct way. As one Schillebeeckx scholar observes, "Schillebeeckx's conviction that the encounter between God and humanity occurs within, but is not identical with, human experience involves a number of subtle and interrelated moves."[24] One of his most frequently mentioned themes is that of the "negative contrast experience" of evil and/or suffering, which

---

21. Ibid., 733.

22. See ibid., 733–43. I have taken the liberty of using more inclusive language than is found in the 1981 English translation.

23. Ibid., 731.

24. Mary Catherine Hilkert, "Experience and Revelation," in *The Praxis of the Reign of God: An Introduction to the Theology of Edward Schillebeeckx*, ed. Mary Catherine Hilkert and Robert Schreiter (New York: Fordham University Press, 2002), 60.

causes the human being to protest against this violation of the *humanum* (what constitutes "livable humanity").[25] From these protests, from these "no" statements to what is, and from imagining what could be, there emerges a basic trust in reality, perceived in fragmentary experiences, that constitutes a "yes" to a better future. This "yes" is where human beings find the promise of God.

To return to Schillebeeckx's list of anthropological constants—while these are characteristic of human experience, they are always connected to, and thus *relative to*, particular circumstances. That is, all human beings are embodied, live in various kinds of relationships, structure their lives in institutions that are relative to their own time and space, and live out their lives in some sort of construct of meaning with both practical and religious dimensions. Like many other postmodern thinkers, Schillebeeckx emphasizes the embodied character of human life, an emphasis that attempts to overcome the Cartesian dualism typical of Western Enlightenment thought. His stress on relationship and on historical conditioning also echoes the postmodern themes of relativity and contextuality. Note that for Schillebeeckx, these constants are always related to a particular context. Like another postmodern philosopher, Martha Nussbaum, who has developed a set of categories for possible human flourishing, Schillebeeckx takes the postmodern situation quite seriously but does not allow it to negate the idea that we as human beings are searching for some kind of meaning.[26] While we live fragmented lives, Schillebeeckx argues that we still search for some kind of meaning, for an affirmation of the *humanum* in the face of the challenges of the postmodern world. And for him, we find that affirmation in the story of Jesus.

Jan-Olav Henriksen and the Other

In a very helpful essay, the Norwegian Lutheran theologian Jan-Olav Henricksen discusses some of the characteristics of the postmodern situation for theology. He stresses a number of the themes I have raised here, including the ideas that there is an "absence of a common human rationality," that "contingency and contextuality are a corollary" of this absence, and that plurality and relativity surround us.[27] All of these

25. Ibid., 64.

26. See Martha Nussbaum, *Women and Human Development: The Capabilities Approach* (New York: Cambridge University Press, 2000).

27. Jan-Olav Henriksen, "Creation and Construction: On the Theological Appropriation of Postmodern Theory," *Modern Theology* 18, no. 2 (April 2002): 157.

postmodern conditions point to a thoroughly "de-centered description of human identity."[28]

But what is key for Henriksen is that "the Christian doctrine of human being *exactly precludes such a centered understanding*" of being human in the sense that the Enlightenment saw the human as the center of the world.[29] Henriksen observes that the Christian doctrine of creation describes the human as created "in the image of God." What this means, he argues, is that humans "have a distinct identity that is grounded in something not positively given, but yet present"—that is, human identity is grounded in its relationship with God. He further points out that

> Christian theology has always made it clear that this perspective of the human being as created is insufficient—even false—when taken to be the sole and only description of what it means to be human. The reason, simply, is sin—which is another way of saying that the human being created in the image of God is not the final word theology has to say about the human.[30]

Henriksen's interpretation, which is characteristically Lutheran in its focus on human sinfulness before God, is a helpful way of showing how the postmodern focus on the "other" has potentially significant theological implications. He makes two important points about this "other": first, it is "given" and "prior" to my existence, and, second, it serves as a "boundary for my own interests."[31] What is particularly helpful for our project is how Henriksen, drawing on the Anglican theologian Rowan Williams, emphasizes the importance of desire. As Henriksen notes, human identity is something for which human beings are perpetually searching: "It is something we are aiming at, searching for, all our lives."[32] Henriksen develops this point further:

> Thus, the existence and maintenance of desire keeps me on the track, allows for further development, further promotion of reflexivity about what I can and should be. That my identity as a human being and as *Imago Dei* is still something to be fully realized, still in the future, is thus not to be considered negatively as a flaw, but as

28. Ibid.
29. Ibid., 158. Emphasis added.
30. Ibid., 159.
31. Ibid., 163.
32. Ibid.

something that makes it possible for us to be liberated from our own instantly self-seeking desire.[33]

For Henriksen, desire is multifaceted: it is the desire for identity and meaning, but it is also the desire for my own gratification. As human beings, we are unfinished and perpetually seek some kind of fulfillment. But if we mistake an idol, something that reflects simply our own desires for something truly other than we are, then we have closed off the possibility of a deeper and more authentic sense of identity. He later notes, "Thus, the human being acquires a more full identity by realizing or being confronted with what it is—and what it cannot yet be."[34]

For the Christian, God is not merely a reflection of oneself and of one's own desires—this is idolatry—but even more, God is not so much "embodied in the world, but represented there."[35] Henriksen's point here is not to negate the incarnation or even a sacramental conception of human existence but rather to stress that God as Other can never be fully known or grasped, never fully embodied, in any one person's experience. Henriksen again quotes Rowan Williams:

> And the absent 'non-existent' third is manifest as the condition for the truthful recognition of my own limits, of the persistence of my incompleteness, because it is not itself *a* point of view, mirroring or competing with mine. . . . Its otherness is radical enough to allow me to be other.[36]

While neither Henriksen nor Williams mentions him, this understanding of one's relation to others where God is understood as a "third" in human experience is remarkably similar to an idea developed by Schillebeeckx early in his theological writings: the idea of God as the "transcendent third" in every relationship.[37]

For both Schillebeeckx and Henriksen, God's transcendence, or to put it in postmodern terms, God's *absence* in the world, is key to understanding the human relationship to God. Postmodern theological critiques of language about God that describes God in objective language, which mistakenly understands God as something to be known alongside

---

33. Ibid., 164.
34. Ibid.
35. Ibid., 166.
36. Ibid., 167.
37. Schillebeeckx, *God and Man* (New York: Sheed and Ward, 1969), 163–79.

other objects, seek rather to maintain God's Otherness in the face of futile human attempts to make God into an ordinary object: an idol. The philosopher Jean-Luc Marion even writes God's name as ~~God~~, echoing the Jewish tradition's understanding that God's name should never be spoken or written, underscoring the impossibility of knowing God.

Karl Rahner and the Desire for God

It might seem odd to the reader that Rahner's name is included among theologians whose work is open to the postmodern. Karl Rahner (1904–84) is a thoroughly "transcendental Thomist" whose metaphysical bent is unmistakable. Following Kant, Rahner stressed the knowing human subject and this subject's awareness of the process of seeking God. In some ways, Rahner could be seen as typical of the problems that postmodern theologians find in the modern Enlightenment model of theology. Rahner relies on both Thomas Aquinas and Kant, who, although very different in time and approach, represent "foundational" (i.e., permanent) ways of doing theology that postmodern critics seek to upset; that is, they assume a stable understanding of reality and a rational self.

In a helpful article, however, Kevin Hogan makes an argument for Rahner's theology as an alternative to "the excesses of the postmodern dissolution of the subject as well as those of post-Cartesian rationality."[38] Like Henriksen, Rahner understands the human being to be grounded not in itself but in a reality other than the self. Hogan argues that "the Rahnerian conception of subject and subjectivity is not that of the Cartesian *cogito*."[39] While Hogan is aware of Rahner's critics, he nevertheless strenuously argues for Rahner's awareness of the need to be attentive to the other, in the sense that his conception of the person is always relational. Quoting Rahner, Hogan writes:

> The only way human beings achieve self-realization is through encounters with their fellow human beings, persons who are rendered present to their experience in knowledge and love and the course of their personal lives, persons, therefore, who are not things or matter, but human beings.[40]

---

38. Kevin Hogan, "Entering into Otherness: The Postmodern Critique of the Subject and Karl Rahner's Theological Anthropology," *Horizons* 25, no. 2 (Fall 1998): 182.
39. Ibid., 191.
40. Ibid., 193.

Moreover, Hogan affirms Rahner's sense that historicity, particularity, and concreteness are unavoidable dimensions of human life, as well as his conviction that human beings are beings-in-the-world, not "being" in the abstract. Finally, Hogan makes a case for Rahner's attentiveness to language and its symbolic character.

But perhaps most significantly for our purposes, Rahner's understanding of the person is that of one who is always asking questions and seeking answers. Human beings have an unquenchable desire to know, and not just to know *things* but to seek and to know the infinite. Rahner's conception of the *Vorgriff*, the anticipatory sense of knowing that there is something beyond the immediate,[41] the sense that our knowledge is a horizon beyond which lies an Other, is central to his understanding of the self. In his *Foundations of Christian Faith*, Rahner describes the human as "man in the presence of absolute mystery."[42] In a powerful and eloquent section entitled "Meditation on the Word 'God,'" Rahner speculates on what human life would be without the word "God"—not just the particular word but all that this word means and implies. He writes, "Man would forget all about himself in his preoccupation with all the individual details of his world and his existence."[43] But even more crucially, "Man would have forgotten the totality and its ground, and at the same time, if we can put it this way, would have forgotten that he had forgotten. . . . He would have regressed to the level of a clever animal."[44] For Rahner, the person is human to the extent that he or she raises the question of one's existence; to be human is to ask this question and to desire to know the answer.

It is at this point that Christian theology and radical postmodern critiques may part company over their understandings of the human person. It is clear that for Rahner the person who is asking this question exists as some kind of unity in the way that asking the question of God provides a grounding for one's existence. Clearly, Rahner's modern existential bent emerges in these passages. But the relational, historical, and linguistic dimensions of human life are central as well.

---

41. Rahner's more technical description of the *Vorgriff*, provided in Hogan's article, is "the transcending apprehension of further possibilities, through which the form possessed in a concretion in sensibility is apprehended as limited and so is abstracted." Ibid., 189–90.

42. This is the title of chap. 2 in Rahner's *Foundations of Christian Faith: An Introduction to the Idea of Christianity*, trans. William V. Dych (New York: Crossroad, 1978), 44–89.

43. Ibid., 48.

44. Ibid.

Concluding Reflections on the Postmodern Self

Christian theological anthropology cannot avoid a serious engagement with the postmodern; in fact, we all exist in a postmodern world, and denial of this is pointless. Certainly, the unitary, rational self in the old scholastic understandings of the "doctrine of man" is, at best, a construction that made sense at a particular time and place and, at worst, one that deprived women and all people in premodern societies of a sense of full personhood. But engagement with the postmodern also raises serious challenges to traditional theological conceptions of the person. Some of these I will deal with at greater length in the following chapters, such as the "essential" masculinity or femininity of the human person. But let us consider a few here.

First, taking social and historical contexts seriously raises the question of whether we can assume that human nature is always the same in every time and place. For example, the individualism of US society is a characteristic widely recognized. So what are we to make of societies that understand the person in a much more communal sense that can even include one's deceased ancestors? Or how does the traditionally Catholic approach of natural law, for example, with its appeal to stable structures of human existence that are true across time and place, find a place in a postmodern world?[45]

Second, liberation theologies and, more recently, global theologies, have challenged the idea that traditional formulations of Christian thought are still adequate for the present. Liberation theologians found in Marx an avenue to understanding the oppressive conditions under which too many humans have struggled. Theologians attuned to the global context ask whether the Christian teaching that Christ is the final and definitive revelation of God can stand in relation to the claims of other religious traditions.

In my view, Christian theology has much to learn from the postmodern critique. I see postmodernity precisely as *a critique*, not an alternative understanding of reality. In other words, the challenges to the stability, rationality, and coherence of more traditional interpretations of the Christian message are serious and need to be met head-on. The message of Christianity is not wedded to one particular set of philosophical/theological categories, even though it emerged out of a particular time and

---

45. See *Human Nature and Natural Law*, ed. Lisa Sowle Cahill, Hille Haker, and Eloi Messi Metogo, *Concilium* 2010/3 (London: SCM Press, 2010).

place. The tradition has adapted its message repeatedly by drawing on the language and ideas of the time, as we saw with Anselm and Thomas Aquinas. While some expressions of postmodernity can lead to nihilism—the belief that nothing has any permanent meaning—its critical questions push Christian theology to articulate the message of the Gospel in ever more relevant terms for the present. The person, in a Christian postmodern perspective, continues to seek God but asks new questions in new contexts.

Chapter Five

The Beauty of Embodiment: Body and Sexuality

In this chapter, we will consider how the desires of the body play a significant role in shaping theological anthropology. Being human inevitably means being embodied. As recent scholars of the body continually say, we *are* our bodies; we do not just *have* bodies.[1] Much of the thinking about the self that we have inherited from our tradition, however, has suggested the latter way of thinking. This sense that our bodies are in some way an appendage to our "real" spiritual or intellectual selves has had a long history in the Christian tradition. Recall that Origen thought that human beings "fell" from a spiritual state to a lower state of embodiment and that Descartes thought that we somehow have to detach ourselves from our bodies in order to think clearly. While Thomas Aquinas took the bodily senses very seriously, the fact that we could not even begin to think without our quite physical brains obviously did not occur to some significant thinkers.

Scholarly thinking on sex and gender has also undergone a sea change in the last generation or two. The most important thinker on this topic has been the French thinker Michel Foucault (1926–84), whose work

---

1. Perhaps the first manifestation of this thinking can be found in the Boston Women's Health Collective 1970 book *Our Bodies, Ourselves*. This book has been revised and reissued a number of times. For more information about the organization, see http://www.ourbodiesourselves.org/about/default.asp (accessed September 17, 2011).

on the history of sexuality has profoundly influenced many contemporary writers.[2] Rather than seeing human sexuality as something "natural" that has a universal and timeless meaning, as much of traditional Catholic moral theology would hold, Foucault argues that we as people in societies *construct* our sexuality in relation to our history and culture.[3] The fact, for example, that in the present, people in the developed world describe themselves and others as being hetero- or homosexual is something that would not have occurred to a person of the eighteenth century and probably does not occur to many people living in some areas in the global South today. The term "homosexual" was developed in the nineteenth century and has come to take on a meaning that would, for instance, have made no sense to people living in ancient Greco-Roman culture. Other thinkers following Foucault have developed this point even further. Judith Butler, for example, challenges the commonly held idea that "sex" is biological and "gender" is cultural; she argues that we are continuously in the process of constructing both our sexed and our gendered identities.[4]

Feminist thought has been a major factor in rethinking sex and especially gender. Feminists point out that theologies of sexuality have been developed overwhelmingly by men and thus reflect their experiences without adequate consideration of how women's experiences may differ. Sex and gender are two distinct but related concepts, as these ideas have been developed in feminist thought and also in the emerging field of queer studies. Notwithstanding Butler's ideas, "sex" largely refers to the biologically "given" dimension of our physiological and genetic construction. For example, as someone born female, I have a set of XX chromosomes, a vagina, ovaries, and a body type that is classified as "female"; my husband has a set of XY chromosomes, a penis and testicles, and a beard—he is "male." When I am asked on a form whether I am M or F, I check F. But what is my gender? Suppose I identify as male, cut my hair short, bind my breasts, and take hormones to produce facial hair. Or, less radically, perhaps I dislike the "traditional" ways that "femininity" is understood, and I refuse to wear dresses, skirts, and makeup.

2. Foucault's body of work is large. His best-known work is his *History of Sexuality*, trans. Robert Hurley (New York: Pantheon Books, 1978).

3. In fact, Foucault makes this point about the nature of all of our knowledge.

4. See, e.g., Judith Butler, *Bodies that Matter: On the Discursive Limits of "Sex"* (New York: Routledge, 1993); *Undoing Gender* (New York: Routledge, 2004); and *Gender Trouble: Feminism and the Subversion of Identity* (New York: Routledge, 2006).

Is my gender still "feminine"? The emergence of the LBGTQ (Lesbian, Bisexual, Gay, Transgender, and Queer) community in the last thirty years makes the usual "male/female" description of human sexuality too simple in its binary division.[5]

Sexuality has also been a topic of much theological attention. Traditional Catholic moral theology has held that in matters pertaining to sex there is "no small matter," meaning that sexual sins are always serious sins, never venial. This attitude comes from the powerful influence of Augustine in Catholic thinking on sexuality as well as from centuries of particular focus on ethical matters pertaining to sex.[6] What it has meant for theological anthropology is that sex carries enormous weight in both systematic and moral theology. It is at the core of what it means to be human. Moreover, the body and sexuality are, perhaps more than other theological categories, areas where *desire* seems to be paramount. Especially in the last forty years, sex has moved to the forefront of cultural and theological attention.

The Body

There are many factors that contribute to a new attitude in thinking theologically about the body, broadly speaking. In the last one hundred years or so, the following movements and events have had a significant impact on Catholic thought. I will simply describe some of these briefly.

1. *Personalism and phenomenology.* In the early years of the twentieth century, the philosophical movement of phenomenology influenced both Catholic and Protestant thinkers. The intent of phenomenology was to draw attention to "the things themselves," so that we pay attention to what is *there* and attempt to avoid placing things, persons, and events in preconceived categories.[7] The goal of phenomenology was to allow things to appear to the observer *as they are*, not as the observer thinks they should be. Phenomenology thus sought to move beyond unchanging categories of thought and to highlight the dynamic relationship between observer

---

5. See Christine E. Gudorf's description of the "collapse of the sexual dimorphism paradigm" in "Sexual Morality in the New Millennium," in *Ethical Dilemmas in the New Millennium,* ed. Francis A. Eigo (Villanova, PA: Villanova University Press, 2000), 29–61. I am grateful to Anne Patrick for bringing this to my attention.

6. See how Augustine describes sins "against nature" in *Confessions* III.8.

7. See Edmund Husserl, *Cartesian Meditations: An Introduction to Phenomenology,* trans. Dorion Cairns (The Hague: Martinus Nijhoof, 1973); and Max Scheler, *Man's Place in Nature,* trans. Hans Meyerhoff (New York: The Noonday Press, 1962).

and observed. Personalism, which sought to define human beings as unique subjects in the world, took a different but related approach. This school deemphasized the traditional Catholic categories of natural law, which tended to see embodiment and sexuality in permanent, essentialist (meaning "of the essence") terms.[8] With an emphasis on the intentions of the moral agent, personalism sought to understand the person as having a unique orientation distinctive to human beings. This meant that thinkers paid attention less to the categories in which things belonged and more to how they appeared, thus highlighting their physical existence.

2. *The Roman Catholic social justice tradition.* Pope Leo XIII's 1891 encyclical *Rerum Novarum* responded to the conditions that had arisen in the eighteenth and nineteenth centuries with the impact of the Industrial Revolution on human life. The encyclical focused on the rights of workers—for example, the right to form labor unions and to receive a "living wage"—and the need to establish decent working conditions and to bring slavery and child labor to an end.[9] Later papal encyclicals in this tradition continued this focus on the need for social institutions to be attentive to the material conditions of human life.[10] While it is probably true that Marxism, among other movements in the nineteenth century, challenged the Catholic Church to respond to its materialist critique of religion, thinkers from Augustine to Thomas Aquinas have been concerned about justice in *this* world, not only in the next. The growth of atheism in the last two centuries, however, prompted a strong response from the church, resulting in an increased emphasis on the point that the *bodies* of human beings, not just their souls, needed nourishment. Social ethics follows from a robust theological anthropology that sees the human as embedded in a society and in a nexus of relationships that constitute the conditions for the possibility of a flourishing life.

8. One moral theologian who advocated a personalist approach was Louis Janssens. See his *Droits personnels et autorité* (Louvain: Éditions Nauwelaerts, 1954). For a collection of essays on Janssens in English, see Joseph A. Selling, *Personalist Morals: Essays in Honor of Professor Louis Janssens* (Leuven: Leuven University Press, 1988). But the most prominent personalist philosopher/theologian was Pope John Paul II. See his *The Acting Person*, trans. Andrzej Potocki (Dordrecht and Boston: D. Reidel Publishing Co., 1979).

9. See Leo XIII, *Rerum Novarum* (1891), http://www.vatican.va/holy_father/leo_xiii/encyclicals/documents/hf_l-xiii_enc_15051891_rerum-novarum_en.html.

10. For a helpful treatment of the papal encyclical tradition on social justice, see Michael J. Schuck, *That They May Be One: The Social Teaching of the Papal Encyclicals, 1840–1989* (Georgetown University Press, 1991).

3. *Vatican II and the turn to the world.* Until the Second Vatican Council (1962–65), Catholic thinking on "the world" often emphasized the superiority of the life to come over the life that we live in the present. It was not uncommon to hear that religious life was superior to married life and that we should mortify our bodies in solidarity with the suffering Jesus. Some Catholics who came to maturity before Vatican II can recall hearing the stories of saints who wore hair shirts and who deliberately put pebbles in their shoes or literal thorns in their sides to inflict pain. (We were encouraged to emulate these saints!) Fasting before Communion stressed that the *real* food we should eat was spiritual, not physical. For the generation that knows only the post–Vatican II world, these ideas may seem either very strange or else very attractive, particularly in a society that seems to have reduced the spiritual to the physical. Vatican II, especially in the Pastoral Constitution on the Church in the Modern World, *Gaudium et Spes,* explicitly stated that the joys and concerns of the world are the joys and concerns of the church as well.[11] This emphasis meant that such issues as war and peace, poverty, women's rights, and marriage were significant religious as well as secular concerns. Previously, "the world" was the province of the laity, while the clergy held sway over the church. Here again, attention to human bodies was highlighted in a way that signaled a new direction for the church.

4. *The Sexual Revolution.* Sigmund Freud deserves a great deal of credit for his emphasis on the importance of a healthy sexual life; the Catholic Church recognized Freud's significance indirectly in Pius XI's encyclical on marriage, *Casti Connubii,* in 1930 and in the following years when authors of marriage manuals rejected the negative thinking on sex that had prevailed in much Catholic theology prior to the twentieth century and voiced the need to develop a much more positive approach to marital sexuality.[12] Furthermore, in *Casti Connubii* Pius XI acknowledged the need for some families to limit the number of children in a responsible way.[13] But it was the development of safe and effective (artificial) contraception that could be controlled by the woman alone (the diaphragm and especially birth control pills) that gave rise to the possibility of

---

11. *Gaudium et Spes,* in *Vatican Council II: The Basic Sixteen Documents,* ed. Austin Flannery (Northport, NY: Costello Publishing Co.).

12. See Susan A. Ross, "The Bride of Christ and the Body Politic: Body and Gender in Pre–Vatican II Marriage Theology," *The Journal of Religion* 71, no. 3 (July 1991): 345–61. See especially 349.

13. See *Casti Connubii* 59.

women having sex for pleasure without the risk and fear of pregnancy. Sex came out into the open, so to speak, instead of being something that was secret and often sordid as well. While natural family planning had been approved in 1930 for Catholics who wanted to limit conception (with the permission of their pastors), Pope Paul VI's encyclical *Humanae Vitae* (1968) condemned "artificial contraception" as intrinsically evil, despite the recommendation of the papal commission that had been appointed to investigate the issue. Now, over forty years after *Humanae Vitae*, the issue continues to cause tension in the Catholic Church; studies suggest that over 87 percent of Catholics disagree with the church's official position.[14]

Since 1973, when the United States Supreme Court ruled on Roe v. Wade, abortion has been the issue that has carried both the moral and symbolic weight of Catholic teaching on sexuality, although the issue of same-sex marriage has recently taken on increased importance. Contraception, abortion, and homosexuality will be discussed more fully in the section on sex below.

5. *The Women's Movement.* The "first wave" of the women's movement began in the nineteenth century and resulted in women obtaining the right to vote in the United States in 1920. The "second wave" rose in the 1960s and empowered women to claim and articulate their own experiences and to seek fulfillment outside as well as inside the home. Betty Friedan's book *The Feminine Mystique* (1963), which gave voice to women who felt unfulfilled in their lives, helped to usher in a new awareness of women's lives and experiences as sources of personal and even theological insight.[15] One of the major contributions of the movement was to challenge the idea that men's bodies were the norm and women's bodies were therefore a deviation from that norm—a belief that goes back as far as Aristotle! Medical experiments that justified particular treatments relied on data almost exclusively from men, since women's bodies, with their hormonal fluctuations, deviated from the "normal" standard.[16] Women came to realize that menstruation, lactation, and menopause were indeed "normal" and that "women's" ailments thought

14. See "Poll: U.S. Catholics Would Support Changes," CNN, April 3, 2005, http:// articles.cnn.com/2005-04-03/us/pope.poll_1_john-paul-catholics-average-pope?_ s=PM:US.

15. Betty Friedan, *The Feminine Mystique* (New York: W. W. Norton, 1963).

16. There is a wealth of material on this topic. For one very good source, see Susan Sherwin, *No Longer Patient: Feminist Ethics and Health Care* (Philadelphia: Temple University Press, 1992).

to be "in the mind" (menstrual cramps, endometriosis, cardiac problems) were indeed quite physical. These medical problems had been previously ignored because men (doctors and the medical establishment) did not recognize their validity since they were not a part of men's experiences or were manifested differently in women than in men, something that is especially true of cardiac issues.

While originally a secular movement for sex equality, the movement soon spilled over into churches and synagogues as Protestant, Catholic, and Jewish women made demands for ordination and other religious roles that were not subordinate to men. Many mainline Protestant denominations had begun to ordain women to the clergy just prior to or in the 1960s. Catholic women also joined in this call for clerical equality. The first Women's Ordination Conference in Detroit in 1975 drew an unexpectedly large audience of women and clergy.[17] But in 1976, the Vatican issued *Inter Insigniores*, which stated that the church was "not authorized" to ordain women, based on historical tradition, its understanding of the will of Jesus Christ, and the complementary relationship between Christ and the church. Despite later statements, such as the 1994 statement *Ordinatio Sacerdotales*, which declared that the issue was "closed" and a fixed part of magisterial teaching, the movement continues in theological conversation and "irregular" ordinations of women up to the present day.[18]

6. *Liberation Theology.* This movement relates both to the Catholic social encyclical tradition and to Vatican II, but liberation theology developed these ideas further into a theology that came to see salvation not as a future spiritual (i.e., disembodied) existence in heaven but as a transformation of human lives here on earth. Liberation theology was begun by a generation of Latin American theologians who had been trained in Europe and returned home to the awareness that the religious questions of the developed world, such as whether or not God existed, were not the questions of their compatriots. Instead, marginalized and

17. See Mary J. Henold, *Catholic and Feminist: The Surprising History of the American Catholic Feminist Movement* (Chapel Hill, NC: University of North Carolina Press, 2008).

18. See *Inter Insigniores* (1976), http://www.vatican.va/roman_curia/congregations/cfaith/documents/rc_con_cfaith_doc_19761015_inter-insigniores_en.html; and *Ordinatio Sacerdotales* (1994); and http://www.vatican.va/holy_father/john_paul_ii/apost_letters/documents/hf_jp-ii_apl_22051994_ordinatio-sacerdotalis_en.html.

oppressed people asked where God was in their suffering.[19] Human beings, liberation theologians argued, cannot consider spiritual things if there is no adequate support for the basics of life and no political, social, or economic freedom, which also have spiritual significance. Thus the poor, disenfranchised, oppressed, body in need of salvation was redefined in liberationist terms.

7. *The Theology of the Body*. John Paul II's development of this maritally focused theology stresses how the body itself is a reflection of God's intentions in physical terms. Men's bodies and women's bodies are created "for each other," and thus their differing psychic and physiological makeup have, he argued, an abiding physical and spiritual significance. This theology of "complementarity" outlined a spirituality and a practice that emphasizes the distinct ways that the masculine and the feminine embody different dimensions of God's plan for humanity. Influenced by the phenomenological movement in his education, John Paul II sought to stress the positive dimensions of the body as part of God's good creation and that human embodiment is a symbol of God's presence with human beings on earth.[20]

8. *The Ecological Movement*. The fact that human actions impact our natural environment and thus our own embodied selves as a part of the natural world is by now a given in both secular and religious thought. The bodies of nonhuman animals and the entire ecosystem are also matters of theological concern. Ecologists are rightly critical of anthropocentric thinking, which assumes that everything important revolves around human beings and that all other creatures are inferior and subject to human action and manipulation. Concern for our bodies inevitably involves concern for what we put into our bodies, so we need to be attentive to farming practices, air quality, the importance of water in human life, and so on. A theology of ecology is by definition a theology of embodiment, as it seeks to place renewed value on the whole of creation. Sallie McFague, a Protestant ecological theologian, has even character-

---

19. The most influential work is arguably that of Gustavo Gutierrez, *A Theology of Liberation: History, Politics, and Salvation*, trans. and ed. Sr. Caridad Inda and John Eagleson (Maryknoll, NY: Orbis Books, 1973).

20. There is a wealth of material on this topic. See John Paul II, *Man and Woman He Created Them: A Theology of the Body*, trans. Michael Waldstein (Boston: Pauline Books and Media, 2006). See also Christopher West, *Theology of the Body Explained: A Commentary on John Paul II's "Gospel of the Body"* (Boston: Pauline Books and Media, 2003).

ized the earth as the "body of God."[21] In a series of books that deals with human ways of thinking about God and the world, McFague has developed a theology that places ecological issues at its center.[22]

9. *Disability Activism.* Until relatively recently, disabled (or differently abled) persons were often institutionalized and/or unable to participate in human cultural or religious life. But in recent years, a number of factors have come together to make it possible for disabled persons to develop a voice and to challenge the conception that their lives are somehow "stunted" or inferior to those of the able-bodied. Educational systems have increasingly made efforts to "mainstream" children who have physical or intellectual disabilities; those who have been born with or have developed disabilities are increasingly able to live longer and more productive lives due to technology and medical advances; and, perhaps most significantly, people are increasingly recognizing that "disability" is a relative term. As human beings live longer lives, we will all probably face some dimension of "disability" in our future.[23] It may be chronic illness, cognitive impairment, or loss of sight, hearing, or mobility. But as the norm of the educated, wealthy white male no longer holds sway, and as we all recognize the diversity of life that is intrinsic to our world, the fact that human beings come in different shapes, sizes, colors, and abilities adds an important dimension to human thinking on embodiment.

All of these factors contribute to a greater awareness of and sensitivity to the embodied character of human being. Thus, the focus of much contemporary theological anthropology sees the body as significant in and of itself, and not as merely the temporary "housing" for our souls. This is not to say that the body has always been seen in dualistic terms; on the contrary, the Catholic tradition has gone to great lengths to emphasize the unity of body and soul. But the emphasis, as it has been heard by the faithful, has more often been on the superiority of the spiritual to the physical. Because God became flesh and came to dwell among us, God was and is embodied in Christ and in the Christian community, and in the earth as well. The sacramentality of the Catholic Christian tradition is based in the incarnation, which means that the materiality

21. Sallie McFague, *The Body of God: An Ecological Theology* (Minneapolis: Fortress Press, 1993).

22. Sallie McFague, *Super, Natural Christians* (Minneapolis: Fortress Press, 1997); and *Life Abundant: Rethinking Theology and Economy for a Planet in Peril* (Minneapolis, Fortress Press, 2001).

23. See, e.g., Joan Tronto, *Moral Boundaries: A Political Argument for an Ethic of Care* (New York: Routledge, 1993).

of human beings and of our world has an intrinsic sacredness. And particularly in recent years, the anthropocentric focus of Christian theology has come under criticism as theologians have realized the impact that embodied human beings have made on the natural world. In sum, to greater or lesser degrees all of these developments have touched on human desires for justice and equality and a sense of personal and social wholeness.

Sex

Sex and Traditional Catholic Theology

Sex is deceptively straightforward: it seems, from a commonsense perspective, that there are two sexes consisting of men and women who are "naturally" oriented toward each other. In (heterosexual) sex, they are able to experience pleasure and to reproduce. Thus, Catholic teaching, going back to Augustine and before, maintains that our sexuality is designed by God for procreation within marriage. Because of original sin—this is a point particularly emphasized by Augustine and that has also cast a long and dark shadow over church teaching ever since—our sexual desires are clouded by "concupiscence," in which we desire our own pleasure and satisfaction.[24] Recall that for Augustine, there was sex before the Fall, but it was entirely rational and only for procreation! After the Fall, however, sex becomes the transmitter of original sin, since there can be no sex without (inevitably selfish) desire. Some later influential thinkers, such as Thomas Aquinas, maintained like Augustine that sex is a good creation of God but also went so far as to say that our present pleasure bears no comparison to that which our first parents experienced.[25] Nevertheless, the overriding sense that sexual desire is always suspect remains a powerful theme in Catholic thinking.[26] Consider that beginning with Augustine (see his *Confessions*), sexual sins are always serious sins, no matter the circumstance. In the later Catholic manuals of moral theology, as I noted above, sexual sins were defined as having "no small matter" and thus were always grave sins. Interestingly, these sections were often in Latin so that only educated confessors could read them.

---

24. See Augustine, *The City of God*, bk. XIV.
25. Thomas Aquinas, *Summa Theologiae* I, q. 98, a. 2.
26. See Joan Timmerman, *The Mardi Gras Syndrome: Rethinking Christian Sexuality* (New York: Crossroad, 1984).

The Catholic theology of sex therefore holds that sexual activity is moral only in marriage and when it is open to procreation, since that is sexuality's "natural" goal. Until the relatively recent past—about the last one hundred years—this teaching was not particularly remarkable. The Catholic Church deserves a great deal of credit for declaring marriage to be a sacrament—that is, a way of encountering God in our human experience—and for insisting upon mutual consent by both partners at a time when women's ability to make their own decisions was hardly common.[27] In the nineteenth century, technological advances made possible more publicly available and advanced forms of contraception; in addition, the discovery of the process of ovulation and fertilization made it clearer how conception takes place. This discovery had an indelible impact on theologies particularly related to conception and abortion.[28] Nevertheless, marriage was often held to be a lesser vocation than the celibate religious life.

There is also what I will call, in contemporary terms, an androcentric and heterosexist bias to Catholic thinking about sex and sexual pleasure. Until the early part of the nineteenth century, it was generally thought that human conception was primarily an act of the male seed finding fertile growth in the female womb. The discovery of the ovum in 1792 and the subsequent mapping out of the process of human fertilization in the next fifty years established the fact of woman's full participation in conception, in that the woman did not merely "nurture" the male seed but contributed half the genetic material of the embryo.[29] Even more, naïve ideas about the male seed "overpowering" the "passive" female ovum have proven to be false pictures of the biological reality. But Catholic moral thinking about sex and sexual pleasure still emphasized the potential dangers of men's sexual appetites and the need for women to keep them in check,[30] and it made little or no mention of women's

27. Theodore H. Mackin, *What is Marriage? Marriage in the Catholic Church* (Mahwah, NJ: Paulist Press, 1982).

28. It is worth observing that the dogma of the immaculate conception was promulgated in 1854, not long after the role of women in conception became known. Moreover, the church's teaching on abortion became much more developed once the process of conception became better known.

29. See Margaret Farley, "New Patterns of Relationship: Beginnings of a Moral Revolution," *Theological Studies* 36, no. 4 (December 1975): 627–46. See also Emily Martin, *The Woman in the Body: A Cultural Analysis of Reproduction* (Boston: Beacon Press, 1987).

30. See Ross, "The Bride of Christ and the Body Politic"; see n. 12 above.

sexual desires.[31] Masturbation, for example, traditionally has been seen as an act "against nature"[32] since the (male) genitals are not used appropriately for their final end, which is reproduction. But what does one make of the reality of female sexual desire and enjoyment, which is centered in the clitoris and which has no purpose other than exquisite physical pleasure? Catholic theology has virtually no recognition of this.

In more recent years, the significance of mutual pleasure has been acknowledged by the church as not only a "secondary end" of marriage but also a part of the "unitive *and* procreative" nature of human sexuality,[33] and the joy and delight of mutual and complementary sex have been emphasized in John Paul II's "Theology of the Body."[34] Nevertheless, the Vatican continues to maintain that any act of intercourse that "artificially" impedes conception is intrinsically evil.[35]

As for same-sex relationships, official Catholic teaching over the last thirty years has consistently emphasized the lack of true mutuality in these relationships. By virtue of the fact that sexuality is oriented toward procreation, homosexual sex is "contrary to nature." The Vatican has argued that homosexual sex is fundamentally "narcissistic," in that there is no physical/sexual "complementarity" between the two partners in the relationship.[36] While the Vatican has come to recognize that same-sex orientation is not a deliberate choice but rather an "inborn tendency," nevertheless, acting on homosexual desires is still "intrinsically evil," and homosexual men and women are counseled to live out their lives in celibacy.[37] It should be noted that the recognition on the part of the

31. See Patricia Beattie Jung, Mary E. Hunt, and Radhika Balakrishnan, *Good Sex: Feminist Perspectives from the World's Religions* (New Brunswick, NJ: Rutgers University Press, 2001).

32. See Thomas Aquinas, ST II-II, q. 154, a. 12, Also see *The Catechism of the Catholic Church*, no. 2356.

33. It was in *Gaudium et Spes* that the Catholic Church declared that conjugal love was ordered both to procreation of children and to mutual love; see GS 50.

34. See n. 20 above for resources.

35. Documents are widely available on the USCCB website (http://www.usccb.org), along with many links to Vatican documents. For *Humanae Vitae* (1968), see http://www.vatican.va/holy_father/paul_vi/encyclicals/documents/hf_p-vi_enc_25071968_humanae-vitae_en.html.

36. See Letter to the Bishops of the Catholic Church on the Pastoral Care of Homosexual Persons (1986), http://www.vatican.va/roman_curia/congregations/cfaith/documents/rc_con_cfaith_doc_19861001_homosexual-persons_en.html.

37. Ibid., no. 12: "Fundamentally, they are called to enact the will of God in their life by joining whatever sufferings and difficulties they experience in virtue of their condition to the sacrifice of the Lord's Cross."

Vatican that same-sex orientation is not a choice but rather a basic orientation of the person is a significant shift.[38] Despite this recognition, though, same-sex activity is still judged as intrinsically evil and contrary to nature as God intended it. It is as if homosexual persons were born with a kind of sexual "disability" that, while regrettable, still does not permit same-sex activity, which remains contrary to natural and divine law. Like the physically disabled person who must adjust to the able-bodied world, the homosexual person is counseled to adjust to this situation and to live without genital sexual expression, which constitutes an appropriately chaste life.

Traditional Catholic teaching remains strongly opposed to the validation of same-sex relationships and particularly to movements for same-sex marriage. As recently as December 2010, US Catholic bishops joined in solidarity with other religious leaders on a statement called "The Protection of Marriage," where they wrote:

> Marriage is the permanent and faithful union of one man and one woman. As such, marriage is the natural basis of the family. Marriage is an institution fundamental to the well-being of all of society, not just religious communities.[39]

For magisterial Catholic teaching, then, to look for validation of same-sex relationships is wrongly to validate something that is out of line not only with the biblical tradition but also with the natural law.[40]

Traditional Catholic teaching on sex has changed very little over the millennia, while scientific knowledge has vastly increased. Catholic teaching remains rooted in the Bible, the tradition of natural law, and, more recently, in a view that sees the relationship between husband and wife to mirror the relationship between God and humanity. My own view is that while contemporary cultural attitudes toward sex are highly problematic—such as the eroticization of human life, even that of young

---

38. See Jeannine Gramick and Pat Furey, *The Vatican and Homosexuality: Reactions to the "Letter to the Bishops of the Catholic Church on the Pastoral Care of Homosexual Persons"* (New York: Crossroad, 1988).

39. "The Protection of Marriage: A Shared Commitment," http://old.usccb.org/defenseofmarriage/shared-commitment.shtml (accessed January 19, 2012). See also http://www.usccb.org/issues-and-action/marriage-and-family/marriage/promotion-and-defense-of-marriage/.

40. This emphasis on the continued relevance of the Bible is evident in the USCCB's statement, referred to below in n. 42, on Salzman and Lawler's book.

children, or the idea that casual consensual sex is no problem—the Catholic Church's teachings have not given sufficient attention to the lived experiences of women and men or to the advances made in knowledge of human sexuality and its diversity. Can one say definitively that no same-sex relationships can be grace filled? Should it always be the case that sexual intercourse be open to (more) children, no matter what the circumstances of the couple? As I will note below, the Vatican's assumption of complete mutuality on the part of the couple may be a positive ideal, but sadly it is not the reality for many women. Given what we know about the diversity of human sexuality, the positive role of sexual pleasure in relationships, and the difficult circumstances in which far too many of the world's people live, a theology of sexuality that is grounded both in embodiment and in justice seems not too much to ask.

Sexuality and Contemporary Theological Anthropology

Especially since the late 1960s, some Catholic thinkers have been very critical of traditional theologies of sexuality. Following *Humanae Vitae*, the 1968 encyclical on "the regulation of birth" (birth control), a number of Catholic theologians took issue with what they considered to be the Vatican's strongly "physicalist" interpretation of human sexuality. Charles Curran, a diocesan priest and moral theologian, is probably the best known of these thinkers. He has argued strenuously over the last forty years for a more nuanced approach to such issues as contraception, masturbation, and same-sex relationships. Curran takes into consideration the overall, not just the biological, fruitfulness of a couple, the loving character of same-sex relationships, and the psychological issues involved in self-pleasure, thus emphasizing a relational and personalist, rather than physicalist, approach to sexuality.[41]

But Curran is hardly alone in his critique of the tradition. Todd Salzman and Michael Lawler, in their controversial 2008 book *The Sexual Person: Toward a Renewed Catholic Anthropology*, have recently argued that "heterosexual intercourse that is mutually freely chosen, just, and loving

---

41. Curran has authored or edited more than one hundred books; to begin, one might start with *Catholic Moral Theology in the United States: A History* (Washington, DC: Georgetown University Press, 2008), and his autobiography, *Loyal Dissent: Memoirs of a Catholic Theologian* (Washington, DC: Georgetown University Press, 2006). Because of his views, Curran lost his tenured position at The Catholic University of America and is no longer able to teach in a Catholic university. He has held a position at Southern Methodist University since the mid-1990s, where he continues to teach and write.

will be deemed moral, whether it is actually reproductive or not, *and so too will homosexual intercourse.*"[42] In a similar vein, Patricia Beattie Jung and Ralph Smith have argued that the real sin requiring attention is not acting on homosexual desires but rather the heterosexist bias that sees all nonheterosexual sexual activity as wrong.[43] Clearly, sexuality is at the epicenter of the Catholic theology of the person. The official Catholic tradition sees "life" issues—that is, anything having to do with sexuality and reproduction—as having a permanent character; these issues have also become the litmus test for Catholicism, particularly with regard to abortion politics, in recent years.[44]

In the second decade of the twenty-first century, it is possible to identify two distinct trajectories when it comes to sexuality and embodiment in Catholic teaching: the more traditional Theology of the Body developed by John Paul II and the theologies emerging from feminist and other theologians who place sexuality and embodiment in a larger historical and social context. In what follows, I will focus first on John Paul II's ideas and then on those of Margaret Farley, a Catholic moral theologian who represents the latter understanding of embodiment and sexuality in Catholic thought.

The Theology of the Body

In a series of 129 lectures given over a six-year period, Pope John Paul II developed a theology of sexuality, gender, and relationship, which has come to be known as the Theology of the Body (hereafter TOB).[45] This theology is characterized by a focus on the specificity of male and female bodies and their orientation to each other, on a relational understanding of human being that sees human beings as "complete" in

---

42. Todd A. Salzman and Michael G. Lawler, *The Sexual Person: Toward a Renewed Catholic Anthropology* (Washington, DC: Georgetown University Press, 2008), 234; emphasis mine. The United States Conference of Catholic Bishops' Doctrine Committee issued a statement in the fall of 2010 that was highly critical of their views. See "Inadequacies in the Theological Methodology and Conclusions of *The Sexual Person: Toward a Renewed Catholic Anthropology* by Todd A. Salzman and Michael G. Lawler," http://www.usccb.org/about/doctrine/publications.

43. See Patricia Beattie Jung and Ralph F. Smith, *Heterosexism: An Ethical Challenge* (Albany, NY: State University of New York Press, 1993).

44. While some US Catholic bishops have refused Communion to politicians who have voted for pro-choice policies (e.g., Bishop Joseph F. Martino of Scranton, PA), others have not. Such a policy is an individual bishop's decision.

45. See n. 20 above.

relation to the opposite sex, and on a vision of human sexuality as reflective of the divine.

In contrast to contemporary theories of sexuality that hold gender to be a social construction, the TOB takes the gendered nature of males and females quite seriously as an intentional creation of God. The spousal metaphor for the relationship of God to humanity and of male to female is central in John Paul II's work and also in other TOB literature. In his 1988 apostolic letter On the Dignity and Vocation of Women (*Mulieris Dignitatem*), the pope writes that human beings achieve unity in the mutual integration of masculine and feminine.[46] There are distinct characteristics to each sex. In particular, a "readiness to accept life" and the "distinctiveness of her potential for motherhood" are central to what it means to be a woman. Much of what the pope writes draws on Mary, in relation both to God the Father and to her son Jesus, as the model for womanhood and also for the church and laity. What is key is how the distinctly masculine and feminine relate to each other: "The bridegroom is the one who loves. The bride is loved. It is she who receives love, in order to love in return."[47] There is a dynamic and mutual relation of initiative-response that is reflected in the masculine and feminine ways of being human.

The male also has its own significance. The pope writes that God's love, as it is understood in human terms, has been revealed in the person of Christ, who is male. Humanity, who receives this love, is therefore symbolized in feminine terms. But only men can represent the essentially "male" (i.e., initiatory) love of God, as it has been represented in the (male) person of Christ. The special nature of women is particularly oriented toward the "care of human life," and all women are oriented to motherhood, whether biologically or not. Thus femininity is fundamentally "receptive," in the thought of the TOB.[48]

The body's "nuptial meaning" is found in the gendered reality of husband and wife, who mirror in their relationship the life of the Trinity. Sexuality is a gift of God to humanity, in which the mutual self-giving of the partners echoes divine life. And, as is the case in divine life, there is no "holding back" of each partner's love for the other; therefore, any form

46. See especially no. 6; http://www.vatican.va/holy_father/john_paul_ii/apost_letters/documents/hf_jp-ii_apl_15081988_mulieris-dignitatem_en.html.

47. *Mulieris Dignitatem* 18. Cf. Susan Ross, *Extravagant Affections: A Feminist Sacramental Theology* (New York: Continuum, 1998), 106ff.

48. See *Mulieris Dignitatem*, especially nos. 16–18.

of contraception in which one "holds back" an element of one's physicality, as would be the case in the use of a condom, diaphragm, or birth control pill, is a failure to live out this total self-giving. A "contraceptive practice and mentality" is the "antithesis of conjugal spirituality."[49]

The TOB has attracted a strong following among a number of Catholics who find in it a positive theological alternative to contemporary culture, which seems to send the message that casual sex is perfectly acceptable as long as both partners are agreeable. The rising numbers of couples who do not find marriage to be necessary, even for having children, and the assumption that an active sex life with whomever and whenever one chooses is the norm are evidence of a highly sexualized culture that extends even to young children. The TOB's sense of the sacredness of sexuality offers a theological and biblical response to a culture of casual sex.

Yet there are elements in this theology that can give one pause, especially for this Catholic feminist. The idea that every sexual act must be open to potential conception does not find resonance among a large majority of Catholics. The point about marriage being "fruitful" is a point well taken, but not every couple is capable of welcoming many children. As Curran and others have argued, fruitfulness does not need to be measured only by one's progeny. But even more than this, the idea that there is a "feminine" and "masculine" essence to women and men, rooted in both biology and psychology, does not find much empirical grounding. We are still in the early stages of knowing how our sexuality is related to both our biology and our sociality. Cristina Traina, a Catholic feminist theologian, writes powerfully about the difficulties involved in applying the papal understanding of marriage to her own experience.[50] While the TOB takes the body seriously, one wonders to what extent the experiences of women have been given sufficient hearing, how the assumption of men's "natural" leadership affects the potential for healthy marriages, and whether the "maternal" nature attributed to all women is in fact so widely shared.

---

49. Christopher West "John Paul II's Theology of the Body: Key to an Authentic Marital and Family Spirituality," http://www.christopherwest.com/page.asp?ContentID=76 (accessed January 19, 2012). West is quoting John Paul II.

50. Cristina L. H. Traina, "Papal Ideas, Marital Realities: One View from the Ground," in *Sexual Diversity and Catholicism: Toward the Development of Moral Theology*, ed. Patricia Beattie Jung and Joseph Andrew Coray (Collegeville, MN: Liturgical Press, 2001).

Margaret Farley and "Just Love"

One of the most articulate Catholic theologians on the issue of sexuality, in my view, is Margaret Farley. In her book *Just Love: A Framework for Christian Sexual Ethics*, Farley explores the question "When is sexual expression appropriate, morally good and just, in a relationship of any kind?"[51] Acknowledging the questions that postmodern theorists raise about the person, Farley nevertheless argues that "we cannot reasonably assert either that we know nothing at all about the human person as person, or that we have nothing of a shared knowledge in this regard."[52] In other words, while human beings differ across time and culture, there are nevertheless certain relatively stable features of human life that are common to all people. For Farley, *autonomy* and *relationality* are keys to understanding the person. That is, all human beings have a capacity for free choice (autonomy) but are, at the same time, embedded in relationships with others (relationality). Farley describes these two dimensions as "obligating features of personhood," in that we are able both to make choices and reflect on them, to determine the direction of our lives, but at the same time we are "not bounded, not complete in ourselves once and for all. . . . We remain radically open to union with others."[53]

Justice, as the title of her book indicates, is the framing feature for her view of sexual ethics. Departing from more traditional understandings of sexuality, which define it as the procreative dimension of human beings understood within a complementary view of marriage, Farley argues that "the concrete reality of the beloved" must stand as the criterion for a love that is just. In other words, Farley does not begin with a theological anthropology that sees men and women as complementarily oriented toward each other, as does John Paul II's Theology of the Body, where men are essentially *active* and women are essentially *receptive*. In the magisterial understanding, human sexuality has an "essential" meaning across time and culture. What is most important for Farley, however, is that human sexuality operates on a basis that has "respect for the autonomy and relationality that characterize persons as ends in themselves, and hence respect for their well-being."[54]

51. Margaret A. Farley, *Just Love: A Framework for Christian Sexual Ethics* (New York: Continuum, 2006), 207.

52. Ibid., 211.

53. Ibid., 213.

54. Ibid., 231.

Farley is appreciative of the views of scholars such as Foucault who challenge understandings of sexuality as fixed. Nevertheless, she argues that it is imperative to recognize the "concrete reality of human persons," which is not always subject to social definition. But her criterion for sexuality, in distinction to the papal understanding of its mirroring the divine relationality, is justice. "Just sex," she writes, involves particular norms that are applicable to all sexual relationships. These norms are (1) do no unjust harm, (2) free consent, (3) mutuality, (4) equality, (5) commitment, (6) fruitfulness, and (7) social justice.[55] It is impossible to discuss all of the implications of these norms here, and the reader is encouraged to explore them more fully in Farley's book. What we should note, however, is that she does not rule out the potential for "just sex" in same-sex relationships. She argues that "the key question is not whether same sex relationships can be ethically justified, but what must characterize these relationships when they are justified."[56] Thus, there is *one sexual ethic* for all relationships, and it is not based on the "natural" or biological capacities of the human but rather in justice.

Another significant dimension of Farley's book is her focus on the social and cultural context of human sexual relationships. Farley is especially aware of the gender inequalities that exist everywhere in the world and particularly in the ways that they affect relationships between men and women in the global South.[57] In contrast to much of the magisterial tradition, which understands sexuality as an "essential" and fixed dimension of human life, Farley takes seriously the differing ways that cultures across the world understand sexuality. For example, she notes that in the African context, "sexuality is primarily for the sake of the community."[58] While there are many positive dimensions to this, there are also consequences that are especially harmful to women. Gender "disparities," which most often mean that men have more power than women and that women's bodies are not their own, mean that one cannot assume the kind of mutuality that is central to the TOB. What is key in feminist understandings of sexuality is women's integrity and ability to make choices about their own sexual desires and actions, something that has always been assumed for men.

55. Ibid., 215–32.
56. Ibid., 288.
57. Ibid., chap. 3.
58. Ibid., 79.

Sex and Sexual Variation

Another important issue to raise is that biological sex is in fact far more complicated than the simple picture of humanity being evenly divided between men and women who are oriented to each other. As a number of scholars note, our sexuality is better understood as falling along a kind of continuum. A small but not insignificant percentage of babies are born with ambiguous sexual organs. Most often, these ambiguities become "resolved" through surgery, with physicians and parents making a determination that a child will be male or female, despite a lack of a clear indication one way or the other.[59] Intersex babies are seen as presenting pathological conditions that must be corrected with surgical practices that can cause tremendous physical and psychological pain later in life when the person discovers that his or her own sexual feelings do not "match" his or her gender. As Natalie Weaver writes, "If the human is the *imago dei* in creation, one must conclude that this image is in all humans. . . . If intersexed persons bear the image of God, then is it worthwhile to consider that God bears the image of the intersexed?" She continues: "And the lesson here? That God is the font of diversity, variety, and newness. That disability, non-conformity, and bodily challenges are also intimate to God."[60] Sexual indeterminacy is an area that has received little attention from Christian theologians and ethicists and deserves far more investigation.[61]

Conclusion

Certainly the sexual revolution of the last century and the eroticization of much of human life over the last fifty years is a very mixed heritage for Catholics today. It is difficult to avoid the impression, if one pays attention to the media at all, that sexual activity is central to human life and that maximum personal pleasure is its main goal. To develop a physically and psychologically healthy sexuality that also reflects the sacredness of the body is a genuine challenge for the contemporary Christian. How is it possible to move forward?

59. See Natalie Kertes Weaver, "Made in the Image of God: Intersex and the Decentering of Theological Anthropology," paper presented at the Annual Meeting of the Catholic Theological Society of America, June 9, 2010, Cleveland, OH. I am grateful to Natalie for sharing her paper with me.

60. Ibid., 19.

61. See Susannah Cornwall, "Sex and Uncertainty in the Body of Christ: Intersex Conditions and Christian Theology," *Religious Studies Review* 37, no. 2 (2011).

While the Catholic tradition has been the object of much scorn for its views on sexuality, particularly with the explosion of revelations in recent years of sexual abuse of minors on the part of the clergy and the scandalous cover-ups of these abuses on the part of bishops, there remains a great deal of wisdom to rediscover in the tradition as a whole. Catholicism's fundamentally sacramental view of reality, based in the incarnation, where God is found not above or apart from but deeply within the concrete lives of human beings, is one such place of wisdom. Unfortunately, this sacramentality often finds itself up against a deeply rooted suspicion of sexual and bodily desires. Historians of sexuality note that there were often proscriptions against sexual activity on a number of days of the week (leading to the phrase "Thank God it's Tuesday!"), suggesting that sex ought to be distanced from any religious activity.[62] Similarly, ideas that sexual desire must always be coupled with a willingness to accept pregnancy seem to come from those who have never had the experience of knowing one's limits with regard to family size.

Yet it must also be said that contemporary cultural mores have come to see sexuality as an individual recreational right: as long as there is mutual consent, there is no problem, since "no one will be hurt." But this approach also seems to have a sadly truncated view of the significance of sexuality for the whole person. Are "hooking up" and/or having "friends with benefits" authentic ways of respecting another person's concrete reality, as Farley asks? Can they lead to living out a committed and fruitful sexuality? The norms that Farley suggests can go a long way in taking seriously our deeply human sexuality and showing how it can be a revelatory experience. Human sexual desires have both potentially positive and negative dimensions.

Feminist thought has been a significant contributor to a renewed and just theology of sexuality. It has revealed the deeply androcentric bias of much of traditional moral theology's focus on male sexual activity and pleasure. For men, pleasure and procreation are linked, where the picture is not so clear for women, as I suggested earlier. In addition, the recognition of the *context* of women's sexual lives is necessary. The issue of women and reproduction provides one example.

By the early 1970s, when "safe and effective" forms of abortion became available and as it became legal in the United States and in many

62. Joan Timmerman, *Sexuality and Spiritual Growth* (New York: Crossroad, 1993). One droll commentator on Catholicism and sex says that for the Catholic Church, "the best sex is no sex."

other parts of the world, the Catholic Church consistently condemned the practice and its legalization.[63] In more recent years, significant pressure has been placed on Catholic politicians who have voted to maintain legal abortion. Both secular and religious feminist scholars, however, have argued that the *context* in which a woman becomes unhappily pregnant should also be taken into consideration. That is, while the assumption of the church is that sexual intercourse is a mutual and loving act, in many parts of the world, women have virtually no say at all in their sexual lives. This is a point that Farley emphasizes in her book. Patriarchal societies frown upon women being other than their husbands' sexual property, and the possibility of using natural family planning and abstaining from intercourse during fertile times can be a very difficult, if not impossible, process when there is little access to thermometers and when culture and daily life do not allow for the time and cooperation of both spouses. The issue of women's sexual consent is a life-and-death issue in parts of the world where levels of HIV/AIDS infection are high; indeed, there are studies showing that marriage itself is a risk factor for women.[64] This example is meant not to justify abortion but to place it within its experiential context, as has been the case with moral considerations of killing done in wars.[65] Women's sexuality has been for too long understood within a context that sees the male as the norm.

Other dimensions of our embodied existence need similar attention. In the United States, we live in a culture that incites desires and pushes for instant gratification. In all of our media—television, internet, wireless devices—we are constantly presented with images that play on our desires for young and thin bodies, for the latest in fashion, for instant answers, for high-calorie foods, for fast cars, and the list could go on and on. Surely many of our desires are normal: for food, shelter, love, meaningful work, and beauty in our lives. But where do we draw the line when it comes to the temptation to go to the mall or to open a package of ice cream when we are feeling bored or depressed? To live a healthy embodied and sexual life is very difficult.

---

63. I use the words "safe and effective" knowing that this means "safe and effective" for the woman who seeks an abortion; abortion is hardly "safe and effective" for the developing fetus.

64. See Melissa D. Browning, *Patriarchy, Christianity, and the African HIV/AIDS Epidemic: Rethinking Christian Marriage in Light of the Experiences of HIV Positive Women in Tanzania* (PhD dissertation, Loyola University Chicago, 2011).

65. Christine E. Gudorf, "To Make a Seamless Garment, Use a Single Piece of Cloth," *Cross Currents* 34, no. 4 (Winter 1984–85): 473–91.

An adequate theological anthropology takes seriously the biological and social experiences of all people—women and men, gay and straight, transgender and intersex—and considers how the personal, social, and sexual dimensions of their lives may more fully reveal "the glory of God as the [human being] fully alive."

Chapter Six

The Human Capacity for Evil and the Hope for Salvation

My God, my God, why have you abandoned me? . . . A pack of evildoers closes in on me. . . . They stare at me and gloat. . . .
—*Psalm 22*

Up to now, this book has focused largely on the ways in which human beings have desired God, each other, knowledge, pleasure, and meaning. I have noted as well where our desires can trip us up, where we can be distracted by desires for lesser realities, and where we can come to disappointment. Sin, as we have seen, is an inevitable dimension of human existence. But there is no denying the fact, especially in the twenty-first century, that human beings are also capable of monstrous evil. How can we hold together a picture of the highest accomplishments of humanity—one thinks of great works of art, the compassion shown by selfless humanitarians, the power of organizations to do good—with the fact of torture, genocide, and rape? How do we make sense of the terrible things that human beings do to each other? In this chapter, I cannot promise that the mystery of evil will be solved—evil remains at its root a deep mystery, a surd, a black hole, the complete absence of God. I hope, though, that an exploration of some of the dimensions of the evil that human beings wreak on each other might suggest a more adequate perspective on what it means to be a human being in the Christian tradition today.

I will focus in this chapter on the evils that humans perpetrate on each other. This dimension of evil is sometimes referred to as "moral evil," as distinct from "premoral," "ontic," or "physical" evil, terms that refer to evil occurrences outside of the direct control of human beings, such as natural disasters and illnesses. I will not be focusing on the issue of "theodicy," which asks how a good and all-powerful God can allow evil to exist in the world created by this God, because the theodicy question is really a question about God and whether God's ultimate power and goodness can coexist.[1] The focus of this work is the human person, and so I will explore ways in which human beings are implicated in doing deliberate evil. Of course the question of God and the question of the human being are intrinsically related, but the question of theodicy goes in a direction that I will not pursue here. The ultimate source and meaning of the existence of evil remains a profound mystery, but the fact that human beings torture, rape, and kill each other cannot pass unnoticed or be simply relegated to the category of an unsolvable mystery; rather, it requires comment, exploration, meditation, and serious grappling. I often hear the phrase "Everything happens for a reason" from my students. Yes, things happen for a reason, but sometimes the reasons are terrible.[2] If there is hope for human redemption, then we must face what requires redemption.

As we have seen in previous chapters, original sin is the situation in which we find ourselves: as both called to life with God and yet unable to respond (fully) to God's call to us. We are finite, yet we are called to an infinite destiny. We are unable to do what we want to do, as St. Paul laments, and we do what we would rather not do. As the myth of Eden has it, there is a serpent in the lovely garden in which we live. Evil is inevitably connected with original sin, yet the two are not identical. I will make a distinction here that emphasizes (1) the human *situation* as one in which (original) sin exists and (2) human *acts of evil*, which occur when human beings inflict evil on each other or stand by and do nothing when they see acts of evil taking place. Obviously there is a connection between the two, but the distinction helps us to focus on human actions rather on than the situation. Sometimes theologians refer to the former

---

1. Recent studies in theodicy include David B. Burrell, *Deconstructing Theodicy: Why Job Has Nothing to Say to the Puzzled Suffering* (Grand Rapids, MI: Brazos Press, 2008); Eric Carlton, *Dancing in the Dark: Reflections on the Problem of Theodicy* (Madison, NJ: Fairleigh Dickinson University Press, 2005); Jacob H. Friesenhahn, *Trinity and Theodicy: The Trinitarian Theology of Von Balthasar and the Problem of Evil* (Burlington, VT: Ashgate, 2011); William Hasker, *The Triumph of God over Evil: Theodicy for a World of Suffering* (Downers Grove, IL: IVP Academic, 2008); and Terrence W. Tilley, *The Evils of Theodicy* (Eugene, OR: Wipf and Stock Publishers, 2000).

2. I am indebted to William George for this observation.

as (original) sin and the latter as (mortal, venial, or serious) sins. This is a helpful distinction as well, but my focus here on the latter is somewhat more narrow: those acts which could be classified as truly evil. In these situations, evil takes on something of a life of its own. Consider perhaps the greatest evil of the twentieth century—the Nazi Holocaust. I only add "perhaps" because comparison of monstrous evils seems absurd. Which was the worst: the Cambodian killing fields, the Nazi Holocaust, the Rwandan genocide, or the Armenian genocide? Millions of people were tortured and murdered in World War II by people who considered themselves Christian, and millions more who also considered themselves Christian cooperated or did nothing while this Holocaust took place. Or consider the Rwandan genocide of the 1990s: Christians turned on each other and murdered each other because of their ethnic identity. Events like these take one's breath away—or ought to. But I want to go beyond standing with our mouths agape and think about what we can say about those who perpetrate evil on others, the victims of evil, and those of us who are witnesses to evil, who may not be directly involved but who share, in near or distant ways, some responsibility.

First, I want to consider briefly some recent writing on the human propensity for evil and how it may well be intertwined with our evolutionary makeup. I will then turn to consider how it is that human beings are capable of doing terrible things to others. My point here is that it is too easy to simply dismiss evildoers as terrible exceptions to the norm, unworthy of anything except condemnation. Next, I want to consider what the effects of evil are on people—for example, what does it do to a person's sense of humanity to survive child abuse, torture, or slavery? While I cannot go into detail, I want to consider what kinds of effects evil can have on the person and how it can affect a person's ability to live and to love fully. Finally, I will examine how it is that human beings can witness evil and find themselves incapable of doing anything to counter it. In all of this, I want to consider whether the theme that we have been following in this book—that human beings are creatures of desire—helps to shed light on the existence of evil in human lives. I also want to investigate what this says about our relationship with God and each other and about our hope for salvation.

The Human Capacity for and Propensity to Evil

Where does our capacity for evil come from? Put bluntly, why do people do terrible things to each other? There is much wisdom in the traditional understanding of original sin that suggests that we are all "born with it," even though we may want to resist the idea that even babies and young children are infected with original sin. A colleague once recounted how her students resisted the Augustinian notion that even children were affected by original sin. She then showed them a clip from *America's Funniest Home Videos* that showed two little girls at an Easter egg hunt. One was happily picking up eggs from their hiding spots while the other was stealthily taking them out of the first one's basket without her noticing. Readers with children might reflect on their own experiences. Or recall the novella *Good Will*,[3] described in the first chapter, where the couple did everything to ensure as perfect a situation for their son as possible, but they still found that they could not prevent evil. Augustine describes the jealousy of babies when their mother is nursing another. All of us probably recognize such tendencies in ourselves and know where our own sinful Achilles' heels are. But when does one cross the line from "garden-variety" human finitude and sinfulness to doing terribly evil things to others?

Human Beings, the Sciences, and Evil

Marjorie Hewitt Suchocki, a process theologian, has given this issue a great deal of thought; her book *The Fall to Violence: Original Sin in Relational Theology* was written after her experience on a jury when she found herself haunted by questions about the human propensity to evil. She makes the argument that "a bent toward violence is woven into the fabric of our humanity."[4] This "bent" comes from many sources: how we have evolved, both physically and socially, over the millennia; our relationships with others; and the "social structures that shape the formation of consciousness and conscience."[5] Violence, as she understands it, is fundamentally "the destruction of well-being."[6]

Drawing on studies in evolutionary biology, Suchocki cites scholars such as Christopher Wasserman, who "developed the thesis that human survival necessarily entailed violence, but that the violence itself was ambiguous, yielding life-enhancing as well as life-destroying behavior."[7]

---

3. Jane Smiley, *Ordinary Love and Good Will: Two Novellas* (New York: Knopf, 1989).

4. Marjorie Hewitt Suchocki, *The Fall to Violence: Original Sin in Relational Theology* (New York: Continuum, 1994), 13.

5. Ibid., 85.

6. Ibid.

7. Ibid., 91.

Because humans learned both to domesticate animals and to use them as food sources—inevitably involving violence—and developed social structures that valued kin relations over outsiders, Wasserman comes to the conclusion that "there is no living species without violent behavior."[8] Building on Wasserman's work, Suchocki acknowledges the persistence of violence in human civilization but then focuses on the development of the human capacity to transcend violence. She comments that a certain level of human consciousness is necessary to be able to identify particular actions as sinful and not only as violent or aggressive. Relying on one of the great nineteenth-century theologians, she says that "Schleiermacher argued that without spirituality, there is no sin. My claim is that without the ability to transcend our violent tendency, there may be evil, but it is not yet sin."[9] From a theological perspective, we need also to remember that this "ability to transcend our violent tendency" can only come from God.

For our purposes, the point is that violent tendencies are, to some extent, part of our makeup as human beings. These tendencies evolved over millennia, but so did the human capacity to understand the effects and significance of violence and to resist it. The next chapter will consider in greater detail the contributions of science to understanding the human person, but it is worth noting here that theologians need to take account of what evolutionary scientists have learned—as we saw in the chapter on sex and gender—about what it means to be human.

In a very helpful article surveying the literature on the human tendency to evil, Stephen Duffy considers how theologians ought to draw on the insights of scientists.[10] While on the one hand he rejects a "wholly biological explanation" of this tendency, he nevertheless argues that "deeply rooted within the human being is a proclivity to evil that conduces to a moral impotency which leads to personal disintegration and social disorder. This can be healed only by grace."[11] While he says that there is a "reptilian core in the human brain," this is not a "genetic program." Science cannot fully explain why some people are capable of doing terrible evil and some of great good; we must be careful of "scientism," which offers simplistic and reductive explanations for complex

8. Ibid., 92.

9. Ibid., 94.

10. Stephen J. Duffy , "Genes, Original Sin and the Human Proclivity to Evil," *Horizons* 32, no. 2 (Fall 2005): 210–34.

11. Ibid., 211.

realities, such as suggesting that we have evolved into violent creatures.[12] Like Suchocki, Duffy argues that evolution shaped human nature so that the conditions both for violence and for moral ideals appeared. We are subject to sin and evil as part of our human condition, but, he notes, we also have choices. We are affected by our social circumstances—that is, we may grow up in a situation where violence is the norm, where impulse control is nearly absent, and where hostility may be the typical reaction to any perceived slight—but we are also capable of recognizing other possibilities, such as the grace offered by God.

In sum, there seems to be substantial scientific evidence—from socio- and evolutionary biologists, from archeology, from neuroscience—that human beings' propensity to violence is, in some ways, "hardwired" into our makeup. Yet we are not merely the sum of our parts. This tendency to violence and evil exists alongside our capacity for altruism, to take just one other positive example, and is situated within our complex humanity that desires transcendence and knowledge of God.

René Girard's Theory of Violence and Mimetic Desire

The theories of René Girard have received a great deal of attention over the last thirty years from scholars in a variety of fields ranging from literary theory to anthropology to the broad area of religious studies, including biblical fields and theology.[13] Girard argues for what one of his disciples calls a kind of "unified field theory for the humanities"—a theory that attempts to explain the role of violence in all of human history and how it has become entwined with religion.[14]

---

12. In chap. 7 I will discuss work that suggests a tendency to empathy is also part of our makeup.

13. René Girard's major works include *Proust: A Collection of Critical Essays* (Englewood Cliffs, NJ: Prentice-Hall, 1962); *Deceit, Desire, and the Novel: Self and Other in Literary Structure*, trans. Yvonne Freccero (Baltimore: Johns Hopkins University Press, 1965); *Violence and the Sacred*, trans. Patrick Gregory (Baltimore: Johns Hopkins University Press, 1977); *The Scapegoat*, trans. Yvonne Freccero (Baltimore: Johns Hopkins University Press, 1986); *Job, the Victim of His People*, trans. Yvonne Freccero (London: Athlone, 1987); *Things Hidden since the Foundation of the World*, trans. Stephan Bann and Michael Metteer (Stanford, CA: Stanford University Press, 1987); *A Theater of Envy: William Shakespeare* (New York: Oxford University Press, 1991); and *Oedipus Unbound: Selected Writings on Rivalry and Desire*, ed. Mark R. Anspach (Stanford, CA: Stanford University Press, 2004).

14. See Leo D. Lefebure, "Victims, Violence and the Sacred: The Thought of René Girard," *Christian Century* 113, no. 36 (December 1996): 1226–29.

There are two basic elements to Girard's theory: mimesis, or imitation, and violence. Girard sees the desire to possess what others have as fundamental to the human condition. As a literary critic, Girard found this dynamic at work in the great novels and epics of Western civilization. And he also noticed that, inevitably, desiring another's goods leads to violence. Girard pursued the connection between desire, religion, and violence in his most famous work, *Violence and the Sacred*.[15] One scholar sums up the book in this way:

> In Girard's judgment, the conflicts that result from mimesis repeatedly threaten to engulf all human life. Escalating violence renders humans more and more like each other, leveling distinctions and sweeping people up into ever greater paroxysms of violence. Mimesis leading to violence is the central energy of the social system.[16]

Obviously, such a system of escalating violence could not continue uninterrupted. Girard goes on to argue that, periodically, societies come to identify a "scapegoat," or victim, to take upon the violence of the community. Then, in a ritual murder, this violence is expelled until it inevitably emerges again. The cycle, he finds, is basic to archaic religions, in which sacrifice is essential to religion. The human roots of violence are shrouded in the myth that the divine demands sacrifice, although in fact the origins of violence are in humanity. One scholar notes that for Girard, "there is no need to posit that humans have an aggressive instinct or a Freudian death instinct. Mimetic desire is enough to account for the appearance of internecine violence."[17]

In his analysis of the Jewish and Christian biblical tradition, however, Girard identifies an important shift. Rather than the victim being the one who is expelled, carrying the blame for the community until the next time, the victim becomes central for Judaism, as in the Suffering Servant of Isaiah and Job, and especially for Christianity, in Jesus. In the latter case, as Leo Lefebure notes, "God appears in history as the innocent victim, who goes to his death as the scapegoat. Far from demanding victims, God identifies with the victims and thus exposes the surrogate

---

15. René Girard, *Violence and the Sacred*.

16. Lefebure, "Victims, Violence and the Sacred," 1226.

17. George L. Frear Jr., "René Girard on Mimesis, Scapegoats, and Ethics," *Annual of the Society of Christian Ethics* (January 1992): 118.

victim mechanism as a fraud and deception."[18] The Christian story shows how Jesus has unmasked the myth of religious violence, that the divine requires violent sacrifice. Girard looks to the Hebrew and Christian Scriptures to show how God, far from demanding violence, in fact is in solidarity with victims.

Girard's all-encompassing theory has passionate adherents as well as critics.[19] A number of scholars question the scope of Girard's theory, as well as his claim that certain "primal" events of violence are the basis for human religion. The interested reader is encouraged to consult both Girard's work and that of his many disciples and critics. Nevertheless, his work raises profound questions about the nature of human evil, questions that need to be asked. Certainly, it adds to the massive evidence that violence and evil are part of our heritage as human beings.

Understanding the Perpetrators of Evil

If one were asked to list some of the worst evildoers imaginable, a very long list would be an understandable result: Hitler, Pol Pot, Osama bin Laden, the machete-wielding Rwandans in the 1994 genocide, serial murderers, suicide bombers, the military torturers at Abu Ghraib . . . the list could go on and on. One merely needs to consult the newspaper every morning for further examples of child abduction or murder or suicide bombings. It is tempting to dismiss evildoers as irredeemable and to consider them as worthy only of relegation to the lowest regions of hell. It is possible to argue that no sympathy ought to be given to those who murder, rape, and torture; "lock them up in prison and throw away the key" is often the knee-jerk response, or perhaps "execute them" through state practices of capital punishment.[20] A 2004 Gallup Poll indicated that 65 percent of Catholics in the United States favor the death penalty, compared with 71 percent of the general population, despite the fact that papal statements and writings from individual bishops and from bishops' conferences have made the point repeatedly, over the last

18. Lefebure, "Victims, Violence and the Sacred," 1227.

19. See Gil Baillie, *Violence Unveiled: Humanity at the Crossroads* (New York: Crossroad, 1997); and Andrew McKenna, *Violence and Difference: Girard, Derrida, and Deconstruction* (Urbana, IL: University of Illinois Press, 1992).

20. At one of the first Republican presidential debates in September 2011, cheers erupted as the governor of Texas, Rick Perry, proudly noted how many criminals (234) had been executed during his term.

twenty-five years, that rarely, if ever, is capital punishment justified.[21] In particular, the *humanity* of those who perpetrate terrible evil is often denied.

My point here is not to engage in an argument about capital punishment.[22] Rather, I want to probe more deeply some potential reasons for doing evil and what can be learned from historical examples. The tendency to simply dismiss the evildoer as a psychopath, wholly aberrant from anything one would consider civilized—"not even human"—is all too tempting. And while there are indeed psychopaths who seem to evidence little if any awareness of or remorse for their actions, as well as mentally ill persons who do terrible things, there is also evidence that "ordinary people" can be capable of evil. Evildoing is more complex than many of us want to acknowledge. A refusal to engage in thinking through the complexity of doing evil means that the potential for repeating great evils is increased, particularly when groups of human beings are involved. As a case in point, I want to take a brief look at the Rwandan genocide of 1994, in which Christians—a majority of them Catholic—murdered over eight hundred thousand of their fellow Christians. I draw on some of the thoughtful literature that emerged after this atrocity to see if we can get beneath the surface of simple condemnation.

One might ask, "Why consider this event, which is so far from the daily concerns of the likely readers of this book?" Africa remains for

---

21. Joseph Carroll, "Who Supports the Death Penalty?" November 16, 2004, www.gallup.com/poll/14050/who-supports-death-penalty.aspx. For formal Catholic statements concerning the death penalty, see John Paul II, *Evangelium Vitae* (1995), http://www.vatican.va/holy_father/john_paul_ii/encyclicals/documents/hf_jp-ii_enc_25031995_evangelium-vitae_en.html. The following statements concerning the death penalty from the United States Conference of Catholic Bishops (USCCB) are available online at http://old.usccb.org/deathpenalty/dpstatements.shtml: USCCB, A Culture of Life and the Penalty of Death (November 2005); Administrative Board of the USCCB, A Good Friday Appeal to End the Death Penalty (April 2, 1999); USCCB, Responsibility, Rehabilitation, and Restoration: A Catholic Perspective on Crime and Criminal Justice (2000); and USSCB, Statement Calling for an End to the Use of the Death Penalty (1980). Also see Chicago Cardinal Francis George, "Lenten Statement on Death Penalty Moratorium," April 19, 2000, http://old.usccb.org/deathpenalty/dpstatements.shtml.

22. For good sources on this, see Cardinal Joseph Bernardin, *Consistent Ethic of Life* (Chicago: Sheed and Ward, 1988); E. Christian Brugger, *Capital Punishment and Roman Catholic Moral Tradition* (Notre Dame, IN: University of Notre Dame Press, 2003); James J. Megivern, *The Death Penalty: An Historical and Theological Survey* (Mahwah, NJ: Paulist Press, 1997); and Helen Prejean, CSJ, *Dead Man Walking: An Eyewitness Account of the Death Penalty in the United States* (New York: Random House, 1993).

many Americans the "lost continent," and the impression one may have is that it is vast, poor, and (although few would want to say this out loud) savage. Having spent time in Africa and, through these visits, having come to a deep appreciation of the African context, I want to question these ideas and ask readers to consider their own tendencies in relation to the issues that loomed so large in this terrible event.

Although it took place less than twenty years ago, many younger Americans are probably unaware of the Rwandan genocide of 1994. A brief summary will have to suffice here; there are many other sources that can provide a fuller description of the situation.[23] For many years there had been tensions between the minority Tutsi ethnic group, who had long held power, and the majority Hutu, with some of the Hutu people claiming that the Tutsi people planned to enslave them. In the years prior to the 1994 massacre, tensions had been increasing. In April 1994, the Hutu president, Juvenal Habyarimana, was killed when his plane was shot down as it approached the Kigali airport. This assassination sparked a violent reaction in which Hutus set out to kill Tutsis, while other Hutus refused to participate in the mass killing. During the next three months, it is estimated that eight hundred thousand people were killed violently, often with machetes. It is also important to note that most Rwandans were and are Roman Catholic.

If there is any one thing that characterizes the conclusions drawn in the literature analyzing the aftermath of the Rwandan genocide, it is *complexity*. This was not a simple event: it had roots in tribal cultures, in colonialism, in the churches, in theology, in human nature. No one of these factors can fully explain what happened, but they were all implicated to one degree or another. Tribal, or ethnic, divisions had long existed in precolonial Africa; each group had its own language, customs, and history, but there was also frequent intermarriage among groups. When the European colonial powers came to Africa, they picked up on these ethnic divisions but made them even more exclusive and rigid than

---

23. For information on the genocide in Rwanda, see Timothy Paul Longman, *Christianity and Genocide in Rwanda* (New York: Cambridge University Press, 2010); Mahmood Mamdani, *When Victims Become Killers: Colonialism, Nativism, and the Genocide in Rwanda* (Princeton, NJ: Princeton University Press, 2001); Gerald Prunier, *The Rwanda Crisis: History of a Genocide* (New York: Columbia University Press, 1995); and Carol Rittner, John K. Roth, and Wendy Whitworth, *Genocide in Rwanda: Complicity of the Churches?* (St. Paul, MN: Paragon House, 2004). The United Nations independent inquiry concerning the 1994 genocide in Rwanda can be found at www.un.org/News/dh/latest/rwanda.htm.

they had been previously, exacerbating differences and minimizing similarities. The churches, for their part, also acknowledged these divisions, often dividing up ethnic groups among themselves or relegating certain ethnic groups to different positions within the churches and thus adding to these differences. Since Rwanda was colonized by Belgium, which has its own ethnic tensions between French-speaking and Flemish-speaking groups, the missionaries who came to Rwanda shared with the Rwandans their own senses of national empowerment and disempowerment: the Flemish-speaking Belgians identified with the Hutu majority, while the French-speaking Belgians identified with the Tutsi minority.[24] In short, the Western/European colonizers found these ethnic differences convenient ways to distinguish among differing groups, but this also fostered rivalry and increased tensions between them.

On top of this, there developed a strong sense of subservience to the church and state. Underlying these attitudes was a deep mythos of national identity. In a powerfully insightful article about the Rwandan genocide and the church's involvement, Jay Carney writes, "In cases like post-colonial Rwanda, the state's *mythos* or foundational story was terribly skewed, with the racist ideology of Hutu power institutionalizing ethnic discrimination and fomenting a genocidal mentality."[25] Carney notes that while the churches, in particular the Catholic Church, were aware of ongoing ethnic tensions, they nevertheless failed to examine these tensions or criticize them. The failure of both the state and especially the church to examine this mythos led to its unconscious assumption and escalation. In other words, the church assumed uncritically the ideas of ethnic identity that had been developed from their ethnic roots, and these ideas became central in church structures, parishes, and seminaries, thereby increasing ethnic divisions.[26] It is worth including a long quotation from Carney's article to emphasize the church's situation:

> To some extent the Church that baptized and educated those who committed atrocities against fellow humanity, bears at least a

24. I am grateful to Professor Veerle Draulans, who made me aware of this situation. Dr. Veerle Draulans is an associate professor of gender studies at Katholieke Universiteit Leuven and an assistant professor in the Department of Culture Studies at Tilburg University.

25. Jay Carney, "Waters of Baptism, Blood of Tribalism?" *African Ecclesial Review* 50, nos. 1–2 (March–June 2008): 12.

26. See ibid., 13ff., for a fuller explanation of ethnic stratification in Rwanda and its role in Catholic life.

measure of responsibility for their actions. This is not to deny the courageous acts of heroism performed by many Catholics during the genocide (priests, sisters and laypeople), hiding their brothers and sisters from the death squads. But in the words of Rwandan Bishop Thadeé Nsengiyumva, "after a century of evangelism, we have to begin again because the best catechists, those who filled our churches on Sundays, were the first to go out with machetes in their hands." One wonders if more Church leaders in the West need to hear such sentiments. Perhaps this would help prevent the Rwandan genocide from remaining a political problem, a human rights problem, an ethnic problem, an African problem, a United Nations problem, but never a *Catholic* problem.[27]

The Rwandan genocide cannot be easily explained as a simple case of ethnic violence. As in other similar situations, such as the Bosnian war in the 1990s, there is a long and complex history that precedes the genocide itself, and, as Duffy, Suchocki, and others would remind us, social structures, culture, and personal responsibility are all intertwined in the situation. There were some who risked or gave their lives to save others, as was shown in the film *Hotel Rwanda*, based on a real person, Paul Rusesabagina, a Hutu married to a Tutsi, who managed to save over a thousand people from certain death. The film shows the terror and desperation of the situation, as well as the refusal of the West to intervene in the massacre.[28]

Since 1994, there have been efforts to engage in reconciliation. The president of Rwanda has emphasized the process of reconciliation, although he too has been criticized for his inability to accept criticism of his own policies. There are moving stories of Hutu and Tutsi women survivors who have joined together in basket making as a means both of reconciliation and of economic development, and of students who refused to divide themselves between Hutu and Tutsi and were murdered for this refusal.[29] While the violence between the two groups has been greatly reduced, the situation remains complex.

My point in drawing attention to the Rwandan genocide is to highlight the complicity and complexity of so many factors: colonialism,

---

27. Ibid., 18; the cited quotation includes a quote from L. Mbanda, *Committed to Conflict: The Destruction of the Church in Rwanda* (London: SPCK, 1997).

28. Don Cheadle, Sophie Okonedo and Nick Nolte, *Hotel Rwanda: A True Story*, directed by Terry George (Los Angeles: MGM Home Entertainment, 2005), DVD.

29. Pamela Sherrod, "The Rhythm of Healing," *Chicago Tribune*, May 11, 2003, sec. 15, p. 1.

nationalism, tribalism, religious identity, and personal and social responsibility. This genocide did not "come out of nowhere"; there were signs pointing to it for years. Could it have been prevented? Possibly, but this would have required the involvement of many parties addressing all of the complex issues, something that seems highly unlikely.

What can be learned from this example? First, there is a serious need to understand and take history seriously. Does this apply to individual people who commit terrible crimes? It probably does. Such persons often have a desire for action: a situation built on pent-up anger, frustration, and a sense of powerlessness. As I was writing this chapter, a Norwegian man who was convinced that Europe was being taken over by Muslims bombed a city building in Oslo and then set off to kill participants at a multicultural summer camp, murdering nearly one hundred people, many of them teenagers. Questions are being asked about the rhetoric of extreme right-wing Christians, about how this man was influenced by this rhetoric, and about the role of violence. What can we learn about what it means for individuals or communities to feel excluded, to be angry at what they perceive to be unjust situations, and to feel powerless about them?

Second, and perhaps more significant for our theological purposes, we cannot ignore the humanity of the perpetrators of evil. This may seem at first counterintuitive: have not those who commit terrible acts of evil renounced their humanity by their deeds? This seems to be the conclusion that many, including many Christians, have drawn. But the Christian tradition holds that all are deserving of God's love and mercy. Perhaps some of the complexity of the evildoer's own background needs to be taken into account. There is evidence that many abusers were abused themselves as children and are involved in a complex process of repetition. I do not seek to absolve the evildoer of his or her guilt but rather urge that we as Christians refuse to dismiss the humanity of the evildoer.

I do not think that any one theory can explain the complexity of violence and evil in the contemporary world. But there are some things that one can learn: the importance of history and knowing a culture's mythos, its self-understanding; the theory of mimetic desire, which may shed light on those who capitalize on economic and social injustices; and the importance of the human desire for revenge. Like other scholars uncomfortable with traditional theodicies, I do not find traditional reasons for the existence of evil to be either convincing or helpful: that is, that God "has a plan," that the just and the unjust will eventually receive their due rewards, or that God is ultimately powerless against evil. The Christian tradition teaches that we are all inheritors of sin and that much evil in the world is a result of human doing, but ultimately evil does not have the last word.[30]

Some individual evildoers are mentally ill; an appropriate response is adequate mental health treatment and protection of the community. Some situations are potentially explosive, as we saw with the Rwandan example. The appropriate response is communal and social awareness of the complexities of the factors involved. Some situations are a result of anger, frustration, failure to take responsibility, or a lack of appropriate education and outlets for such emotions. One thinks of roving gangs of youth who attack others as sport, or gangs that require their initiates to kill someone as proof of their commitment to the gang. One ponders those who take pleasure in torturing people or animals, and at the very least one must acknowledge that there are obviously grave problems with their capacity for empathy.

To be clear: I am not suggesting that every act of evil has a social solution. How some parents can decide that their child is a "monster" and must be beaten, caged, and starved to death leaves me horrified and helpless. But the *Christian* response is not simply to reject evil and turn one's back, to simplify it and set oneself as the good person over and against the evildoer. Rather, evil must be faced and resisted, as Jesus did. Facing evil means trying to understand its complexity and the many factors that can turn a potentially bad situation into a terrible one. Facing evil means refusing the "sound bite" of our culture and being willing to ask what factors contribute to the evil situation's sources and effects. And as we face evil, we are obligated to resist it as best we can. Some do this heroically, like Paul Rusesabagina, or the Ugandan martyrs, or the Trappist monks depicted in the powerful film *Of Gods and Men*.[31] We may not have the opportunity to be heroes, but we can refuse simplistic

---

30. For a powerful theological treatment of evil, see Wendy Farley, *Tragic Vision and Divine Compassion: A Contemporary Theodicy* (Louisville, KY: Westminster John Knox, 1990).

31. Lambert Wilson, Michael Lonsdale, and Olivier Rabourdin, *Of Gods and Men*, directed by Xavier Beauvois (New York: Sony Pictures Classics, 2011), Blu-ray. For more information on Paul Rusesabagina, see Paul Rusesabagina, *An Ordinary Man: An Autobiography*, with Tom Zoellner (New York: Penguin Books, 2007). Concerning the Ugandan martyrs, see Barry M. Coldrey, *The Ugandan Martyrs* (Thornbury, Australia: Tamanaraik Press, 2001); Charles Dollen, *African Triumph: The Life of Charles Lwanga and Other Martyrs of Uganda* (Boston: St. Paul, 1967); and Timothy J. Furry, "Bind Us Together: Repentance, Ugandan Martyrs, and Christian Unity," *New Blackfriars* 89, no. 1019 (January 2008): 39–59.

responses in favor of one that is Christian. It is not an easy response, but the other demands of Christian belief are not easy either.

Victims of Evil

As the readers of this book are well aware, the Catholic Church is still reeling from the revelations that children and teens were regularly abused by Catholic priests and nuns and that too many priests and bishops did nothing, or did not do enough, to hear their cries. We have learned much about the aftereffects of trauma from those suffering from post-traumatic stress disorder (PTSD) as a result of military service in war zones or from traumatic events such as torture, rape, or abuse.[32] Victims do not simply "get over" their trauma in a given period of time: the sense of fear, worthlessness, and despair can linger for years. Increasingly, PTSD and the long-term effects of suffering are becoming better known, and there are more therapies to help those who continue to suffer.

My reason for including a section on victims of evil stems from my awareness that we most likely grossly underestimate the numbers of victims of evil in our midst. I have had a number of occasions in classes when the topics of rape, domestic violence, torture, or some other terrible evil were discussed and a student would come up to me after class to thank me for raising the topic, since the student had personal experience with the issue. One unforgettable moment came in a class on theology and the arts, where we discussed the image of "Christa," Edwina Sandys's sculptural portrayal of a naked woman on a cross.[33] While most of the male students objected to the image as being pornographic, two women students in particular defended it, saying that it gave them comfort in their own distress and healing from abuse and assault, knowing that their suffering was in solidarity with Jesus. In another class, in a discussion of concentration camps in World War II, a student originally from Cambodia referred to his and his family's experiences in the "killing fields."

32. See Jesse Perillo, "The Destructive Nature of Suffering and the Liturgical Refashioning of the Person" (PhD diss., Loyola University of Chicago, 2011); and A. Denise Starkey, *The Shame That Lingers: A Survivor-Centered Critique of Catholic Sin-Talk* (New York: Peter Lang, 2009).

33. See Susan A. Ross, "God as Bride: Toward a Christology of Diversity," in *God, Science, Sex, Gender: An Interdisciplinary Approach to Christian Ethics*, ed. Patricia Beattie Jung and Aana Marie Vigen (Collegeville, MN: Liturgical Press, 2001), esp. 216–19.

In this section, I want to draw on some recent work that shows how trauma can have a devastating effect on one's life and one's relationships with oneself, others, and God. These effects need to be taken seriously by theologians, who may otherwise tend to see such victims as unfortunate exceptions to the norm of what it means to be a human being. Theological anthropology needs to take greater account of the ways that evil can affect human beings as victims.

Trauma Victims

With the growth of feminist scholarship over the last forty years, much has come to light about the suffering experienced by victims of domestic violence, incest, and other forms of abuse. While the victims of these crimes can be male or female, the great majority of victims of domestic violence and of incest are female. One of the oft-quoted comments made by feminists in the early years of the women's movement about such issues is "What we now call 'domestic violence' used to be just called 'life.'" Trauma has a devastating effect on people. For children who suffer sexual abuse, their sense of their own bodily integrity and selfhood is altered dramatically if not nearly destroyed.[34] Survivors of wartime violence struggle to regain a sense of what is "normal" and often respond with exaggerated alarm to noises or threats even years after the original trauma took place.[35] Survivors of torture find it excruciating to resume a sense of normalcy.[36]

A number of scholars have taken on issues of victimization, violence, and suffering in recent years, many of them with feminist perspectives on these issues.[37] One of the first things to note about victims and victimization is the tendency by those who know or are close to victims to

---

34. Jennifer Beste, "Recovery from Sexual Violence and Socially Mediated Dimensions of God's Grace: Implications for Christian Communities," *Studies in Christian Ethics* 18, no. 2 (2005): 89.

35. See Perillo, "The Destructive Nature of Suffering and the Liturgical Refashioning of the Person."

36. Almerindo E Ojeda, *Trauma of Psychological Torture* (Westport, CT: Praeger, 2008); Joshua E. S. Phillips, *None of Us Were Like This Before: American Soldiers and Torture* (New York: Verso, 2010); and Guus Van der Veer, *Counseling and Therapy with Refugees: Psychological Problems of Victims of War, Torture, and Repression* (Chichester, NY: Wiley, 1992).

37. See, e.g., Jennifer Beste, *God and the Victim: Traumatic Intrusions on Grace and Freedom* (New York: Oxford University Press, 2007); Wendy Farley, *Tragic Vision and Divine Compassion: A Contemporary Theodicy* (Louisville, KY: Westminster John Knox Press, 1990); Elaine Scarry, *The Body in Pain: The Making and Unmaking of the World*

either deny or underplay the significance of traumatic events. This was certainly the case for victims of clergy sexual abuse over the years. Victims were told by their abuser that they were forbidden to speak about what happened; children who suffer incest or other forms of sexual abuse face similar warnings, which are often compounded by the denial of other parents or caretakers. Rape is a famously underreported crime. Those who suffer evil in this way often feel terrible shame and guilt about their situation, thinking that they did something to "deserve it," as they may have been told by the perpetrator or abuser, or that they somehow should have been able to prevent it.

Another point to note is that because the Christian tradition has often viewed suffering as a "participation in the suffering of Jesus," the kind of justified anger at a situation of violence and/or abuse may be blunted by the misguided sense that suffering is part of the purpose of a Christian life. The work of Dorothee Soelle has been especially helpful in raising this issue to the fore.[38]

But the more significant points to note for our concerns are the long-term and devastating effects on people and their inability to live a life of freedom and integrity. In a powerful book about freedom and trauma, Jennifer Beste asks whether the theological anthropology of Karl Rahner, one of the most influential theologians of the twentieth century, is adequate to address the damaged sense of selfhood that is experienced by many victims.[39] As a seminary intern in a mental health clinic, Beste encountered a young girl who had been sexually abused for nine years beginning when she was two. The girl was seriously disturbed, and the staff of the clinic doubted whether she would be able to go on to live anything resembling a normal life. Later, as a graduate student in a course on Karl Rahner, Beste found herself asking whether this girl would be able to exercise her "fundamental option," her response to the call that God extends to every person, with the kind of freedom and self-reflection that Rahner presupposed was basic to humanity.[40]

(New York: Oxford University Press, 1985); Starkey, *The Shame That Lingers*, n. 32 above; and Suchocki, *The Fall to Violence*, n. 4 above.

38. Dorothee Soelle, *Suffering*, trans. Everett R. Kalin (Philadelphia: Fortress Press, 1975).

39. Beste, *God and the Victim*.

40. Ibid., chap. 2, on Karl Rahner is quite helpful. For the primary source, see Karl Rahner, *Foundations of Christian Faith: An Introduction to the Idea of Christianity*, trans. William V. Dych (New York: Crossroad, 1978).

Beste considers the question that a number of theologians have asked over the years: Is it possible for evil to render someone incapable of salvation? She notes that the tradition has long held that we all receive from God what we need in order to respond to God's call. As Thomas Aquinas says, "No man dies spiritually except by sinning of his own will."[41] Particularly in the West, the assumption is that human beings are free and self-determining agents. Is it possible, then, that some harm can be so serious that it is impossible for a person to respond to God, that such damage has been done to a person that despair or suicide is the only option that such a person can see? Like a number of feminist scholars, Beste is critical of the high place that reason holds in many accounts of human agency; this is not to say that reason is unimportant, but rather that the power of reason, along with one's ability to engage in relationships, can be so diminished by terrible trauma that it no longer is central.[42]

Beste notes that it is common for trauma victims to survive by fragmenting themselves, by dissociating, by repressing emotional affect—all ways of dealing with trauma that also affect negatively one's ability to reason and to trust one's sense of reality. The abused child must somehow make sense of the fact that the person responsible for her health and well-being is also the source of her terrible suffering. In order to survive, victims often "split off" parts of themselves so as to attempt to blunt the dreadful impact of the abuser's actions. Beste notes that "such fragmentation of the self and compromised categorical freedom challenge Rahner's confidence that persons endowed with reason have sufficient freedom for ultimate self-disposal."[43] Moreover, she notes as well that Rahner's examples of the self who responds fully to God build on the long-held assumption that the fundamental human sin is pride and that self-denial is key to a full relationship.[44] Beste does note that later in life, Rahner seemed more open to the possibility that some—he mentions the example of those "born in chains"—may not find it possible to respond in freedom.[45]

---

41. Ibid., 8, quoting Thomas Aquinas, *Summa Theologiae* I-II, q. 73, a. 8, ad. 3.

42. There is recognition in the Catholic moral tradition that certain "impediments" can affect one's culpability. For a helpful discussion, see Timothy E. O'Connell, *Principles for a Catholic Morality*, rev. ed. (New York: HarperCollins, 1990), 53ff.

43. Beste, *God and the Victim*, 87–88.

44. Ibid., 91.

45. Ibid., 96.

Beste then develops what she calls a "revised Rahnerian theology of grace and freedom" that views grace as always and everywhere a *mediated* reality; that is to say, grace never comes to us apart from our relationships with others and our environment.[46] Grace is not "fairy dust" that is sprinkled on us directly by God. Instead, she notes that "a primary way in which God communicates grace is through the experience of loving, interpersonal relations."[47] While interpersonal relationship can be the source of terrible evil, "human love can also become occasions of God's mediating grace."[48] Beste goes on to develop some of the ethical implications of an adequate recognition of deep trauma and its effects on individuals and communities.

PTSD is another example of the continuing trauma that is endured by many survivors of war and other traumatic events. Today there is greater recognition of PTSD as a genuine disability and also as a treatable—although very difficult to treat—consequence of trauma. As I was writing this chapter, I came across an example of a veteran whose PTSD led him to dangerous encounters with law enforcement and nearly to suicide. Fortunately, in this case a sensitive criminal justice system took account of the devastating impact of PTSD on veterans and allowed him an alternative treatment process that recognized the psychological and emotional dimensions of his actions.[49] Today greater societal attention needs to be focused on survivors of war trauma, and the church needs to take greater account of their suffering and offer solace to victims.[50]

Social Trauma

There are many ways that trauma can affect a community, an ethnic group, or a nation. One could name the Nazi Holocaust, its impact on Jewish identity, and the ongoing divisions with the Palestinian people; the long struggle against South African apartheid and its continuing effects on South Africans of all races and ethnic groups; and, as we saw above, the Rwandan genocide, its roots in history, and its continuing impact on the country. But perhaps no communal trauma has had as longstanding an effect on a whole group of people as that of slavery and

46. Ibid., 105.
47. Ibid., 104.
48. Ibid., 105.
49. Erica Goode, "Coming Together to Fight for a Troubled Veteran," *New York Times*, July 18, 2011, A1.
50. See Perillo, "The Destructive Nature of Suffering and the Liturgical Refashioning of the Person."

its accompanying evil of racism, especially as it is experienced in the United States. Racism is something that many white people would like to think is a thing of the past. With the election of an African American man to the US Presidency in 2008, some have argued that we are now in a postracist society.

But it is dangerous to jump to this conclusion too quickly. While slavery is no longer (visibly) practiced in the United States—I make this qualification because of the continuing tragedy of the sex trade, which can be described as a modern form of slavery, and various forms of indentured servitude that are by any definition slavery—racism is "as American as mother's milk," as one saying goes. Many white Americans tend to see racism as a problem experienced by black people and made worse by certain very prejudiced white people, certainly not themselves. For their part, the victims of racism are keenly aware of the large and small slights experienced on a daily basis; white people need to become aware of the "privilege of whiteness," a sense that their own racial and embodied experience is seen as the norm, and that this poses grave problems.[51] I live in a middle-class suburb outside Chicago, and on occasion my husband and I drive with our dogs to a nearby wealthy suburb to go for a walk on a weekend afternoon. I often think how we are, in a sense, invisible in these wealthy neighborhoods: a white couple walking their dogs. How unremarkable. If we were black, would we be able to walk these same neighborhoods without attracting negative attention? I doubt it. But attention to race in particular and to the many other dimensions of our embodied selves—sex, culture, ethnicity—is necessary.

One of the foremost writers on this issue is M. Shawn Copeland, who observes in her book *Enfleshing Freedom: Body, Race, and Being* that "absolutizing or fetishizing what can be seen [i.e., race, sex, culture] . . . risks 'fragmenting' the human being. But what makes such risk imperative is the location and condition of bodies in empire; what makes such a risk obligatory is that the body of Jesus of Nazareth, the Word made flesh, was subjugated in empire."[52] Copeland's point is that in the present US context, with its "breathtaking self-designation as the world's

---

51. On the issue of the "privilege of whiteness," see Jon Nilson, *Hearing Past the Pain: Why White Catholic Theologians Need Black Theology* (New York: Paulist Press, 2007); and Laurie M. Cassidy and Alexander Mikulich, *Interrupting White Privilege: Catholic Theologians Break the Silence* (Maryknoll, NY: Orbis Books, 2007).

52. M. Shawn Copeland, *Enfleshing Freedom: Body, Race and Being* (Minneapolis: Fortress Press, 2010), 57.

sole superpower," it is imperative to take bodies seriously, particularly when this context is in such contrast to the reign of God preached by Jesus of Nazareth.[53]

The evils of slavery were multiple: individuals and families were not only torn away from their homeland and from each other; they were also torn away from the long stream of familial and generational connections that the African tradition of the veneration of ancestors has long honored. As Copeland, drawing on Orlando Patterson, has noted, "the captured were now among the dead who still lived."[54] People became commodities whose only purpose was back-breaking work or "breeding." Subject to brutal beatings, as well as separation from spouses and children, slaves were not seen as fully human; indeed, they were classified as three-fifths of a person in the original US Constitution.

The abolition of slavery may have changed the official situation for the descendants of slaves, but their lives were still held to be of little or no value in many parts of this country. Jim Crow laws made it nearly impossible for black people to live peaceful, productive lives. Always aware of the potential for suspicion, black families would plan trips so as to avoid overnight stays anywhere that could pose problems—and they were the lucky ones. Those far unluckier were subject to the worst practices of the Jim Crow era: lynchings. It took little to incite a crowd to decide that a black person, often a young man, was guilty of such offenses as whistling at or even accidentally brushing by a white woman, and the response was brutal murder.[55]

But, one might say, these examples are all in the past. Yes, the most egregious and overt examples are largely in the past, but racism continues to infect the Body of Christ. Black applicants are less likely to get favorable mortgage rates than their white counterparts; far too many black youth languish in prisons, and too many white Americans do not see this terrible loss as a problem. Young black children are less likely than their white counterparts to be educated in well-equipped schools, to eat nutritious food, and to go on to receive college educations. Unconscious as well as conscious racism continues to affect all of us—people "of color" as well as those designated to have "no color." As Copeland notes, Christian faith demands that we follow Christ as his Body, and "embodying Christ is discipleship, and discipleship is embodied

53. Ibid., 56–57.
54. Ibid., 111.
55. Ibid.

praxis. . . . Eucharistic solidarity orients us to the cross of the lynched Jesus of Nazareth, where we grasp the enormity of suffering, affliction, and oppression as well as apprehend our complicity in the suffering, affliction, and oppression of others."[56] My point is that the terrible effects of slavery are still with us and demand recognition and response. Racism hurts everyone and is a wound on the Body of Christ.

Witnesses to Evil

We are all witnesses to evil. We hear about evil from news media; perhaps we have experienced some serious evil in our own lives. Every day I learn from the news media about more murders, rapes, and drive-by shootings in my own city. I am aware of the growing famine in eastern Africa; two years before this writing, I saw for myself how severely the drought had already affected the lives of people and wildlife in Kenya. I read about returning soldiers with PTSD, and I also read about how wealthy bankers have profited from unjust and manipulative borrowing practices, leaving millions of people homeless.

How do we respond? Do we take steps to stop evil from taking place? What do we do when we see it happening before our own eyes or impacting our environment? How should a Christian respond? What is our *distinctly human* responsibility? Let me suggest three basic points: witness, resistance, and hope.

To be a witness is to acknowledge the reality of the existence of evil in our midst. It is to say that these terrible things happen. We cannot deny that children starve and are abused by their caretakers, that people are beaten and killed unjustly, that there are terrible discrepancies in income not only in the "third world" but in our nation as well, and that these situations should not exist. As I noted above in discussing victims of evil, one of the worst experiences for someone who has experienced something terrible is to have it denied by others. The witness is the one who is able to speak for others when they cannot speak and to confirm the existence of an injustice. One thinks of the women who stood by Jesus at the foot of the cross. They did not abandon the innocent victim of evil in his suffering. Yet it is also important to note that a significant form of witness is listening. Victims of evil need to be able to speak for themselves, if at all possible, and to have their voices heard.

---

56. Ibid., 128.

Witness can take a number of different forms: making a situation visible, doing something to increase public recognition, writing about it, or simply telling one's friends and family. With the explosive growth of different communication media, one can hardly avoid knowing about events that take place and signing on to a cause. But I suggest the *Christian witness* requires more than a click of the mouse on one's computer. Among the principles of Catholic social teaching are the call for the promotion of the common good, a preferential option for the poor and vulnerable, and solidarity with all of our (human) brothers and sisters.[57] In a highly individualistic culture, it is all too easy to burrow into one's own "cocoon," but the Christian tradition is a communal one. Witness calls us to be in solidarity with victims.

The next step is resistance. While witness is the first step, in itself it is not enough. Resisting evil can take many forms, and not all of us are equipped to take up arms, real or metaphorical, against evildoers. Resistance is also both personal and communal. On a personal level, we are called to resist the evil that can harm us and those close to us. Thomas Aquinas is often cited for his support of self-defense as a valid reason to fight against another person, but not all forms of evil require the use of violence in order to overcome it.[58] We are all called to resist, as far as we are able, the denigration of ourselves and others; this can mean, for example, speaking up when sexist, racist, homophobic, and demeaning comments are made in our presence. It can also mean a call to an agency to protect an abused child, helping to draw up rules that prohibit discrimination, or marching to protest violence against women and children. While in the Gospel of Matthew Jesus calls for "turning the other cheek," what is not as well-known is how this gesture in its cultural context is a powerfully resistant one that uses the aggressor's own power against him. It does so by changing the power dynamics of the encounter by requiring the aggressor to use the culturally forbidden left hand, thereby depriving him of his power to humiliate.[59] Jesus calls us not to be passive doormats but rather to respond as creatively, if also as nonviolently, as possible.

57. For the major themes of Catholic social teaching, see the Office for Social Justice St. Paul and Minneapolis online at http://osj.webaloo.com/major_themes.aspx.

58. See Thomas Aquinas, ST, II-II, q. 64, a. 7.

59. Walter Wink, *Jesus and Nonviolence: The Third Way* (Minneapolis: Fortress Press, 2003); I am grateful to Anne Patrick for pointing me to this text. See her *Women, Conscience, and the Creative Process* (New York: Paulist Press, 2011).

Finally, we are called, as Christians, to hope. Hope is not a pie-in-the-sky wish that everything will turn out all right. All too often, things do not end well. Innocent people die; evil people prosper; cruelty to all forms of life continues without repercussions. But Christian faith in the paschal mystery is faith that because God is with us in our suffering, suffering does not have the last word. The resurrection is the sign of hope that while Jesus Christ died an ignominious death, God raised him up as God will raise all of us up. In the present, we are all the Body of Christ, living in hopeful witness and resistance.

Chapter Seven

Theology, Science, and Human Personhood

As we near the end of this extended reflection on what it means, from a Christian perspective, to be a human being, we turn to the sciences. Although this is a book of theology, it would be both difficult and mistaken to ignore the many scientific findings and technological developments of recent decades that have a tremendous impact on theological understandings of the human person. The Catholic theological tradition is not hostile to science, nor does it take a view of the person that draws only on biblical images, as should be evident from chapter 1. Given the kinds of questions about humanity that the sciences have raised, especially recently, it is worth venturing out of what may be most theologians' comfort zones to explore what scientific contributions or questions may be pertinent to theological anthropology.

The ideas in this chapter are those of a theologian who tries to read broadly and to think about what various fields of knowledge may have to contribute to our self-understanding. In the last few decades, human lives have been profoundly affected by changes in science and technology, many of which have significant implications for theological anthropology. We know more about our surroundings, our internal workings, and our fellow creatures than we did only a few decades ago, and we are faced with issues and decisions about our lives involving sciences and technologies that were unheard of less than a half century ago. So in many ways this chapter is informed by what the great Canadian Jesuit theologian Bernard Lonergan (1904–84) referred to as "the unrestricted desire to know." How are we connected with our fellow creatures? What are the limits to our knowledge of what we can change about ourselves? In our desires to know as much as we can and to do as much as we are able, what would a Christian perspective say about the relevance of the sciences and recent scientific advances to theological anthropology?

It used to be the case, for example, that there were thought to be clear divisions between nonhuman animal life and "us." We reasoned; they did not. We felt compassion; they were dumb beasts. We felt pain; they did not. We were emotionally attached to others; they were not. But research on nonhuman life over the last century or so in many different fields has shown that all the statements above are basically wrong. While our human forms of reasoning may not be shared exactly by other creatures, many nonhuman animals nevertheless can solve problems, feel pain and compassion, and form strong bonds with their fellow creatures and with us. So the question "What makes us human?" is more complex than ever before, for both scientists and theologians.

We not only continue to wonder about what makes us human; we also are learning more about the complex ways that our brains, along with our entire physical organisms, affect the ways we feel, think, and act, including our religious feelings, thoughts, and actions. Neuroscience is an exploding field of study that has shed new light on many things that in the past we may have thought were entirely "mental," meaning existing independently from the physical. Now, the difference between the mental and the physical is no longer so clear. The physiological basis for feelings and drives makes us question older ideas we may have had about the power of the mind over the body.

New technologies are also changing the ways that we think about our humanity. It is now possible to make choices about reproduction that were only in the realm of the imagination just decades ago. We live longer lives (and so do our domesticated nonhuman companions) thanks to advances in science and technology. From the possibility of "reducing" multiple pregnancies to a desired number to preimplantation genetic diagnoses to sex selection through very early blood tests, we face the possibility of "designing" our offspring rather than "leaving it up to God." What kinds of limits should there be in making such momentous decisions?

In this chapter, I will explore some of the ways that science and technology are changing the ways that we view ourselves and our relationship with the rest of creation. Given the Catholic theological tradition's conviction that grace builds on nature and does not destroy it, theologians have an obligation to pay attention to what the sciences say about our humanity, our inner workings, and our relationships to other creatures and to the cosmos.[1] So we ask, should our desire to know and to reach the impossible have any limits? How do scientific advances raise theological questions?

What Makes Us the Imago Dei?

Much of our theological tradition emphasizes the uniqueness of human beings. The psalmist writes, "What is [the hu]man that you are mindful of him?" (Ps 8:5). The first Genesis account places human beings in dominion over all other creatures of the earth. Thomas Aquinas writes that human beings are distinct from other animals because of our rationality, which he assumes animals ("beasts," in Thomas's terms) do not share, although he does credit to nonhuman creatures a measure of rationality that is distinctive to them.[2] It seems to be a religious or, at least, a Christian truism that human beings have a special place in the world, above all other living beings.[3] The suggestion that human beings and the great apes might share a common ancestor has driven biblical fundamentalists to dismiss any theory of evolution as contrary to biblical truth. Yet what do we do with the scientific evidence that we share over 96 percent of our genes with chimpanzees? The pages of both learned and popular scientific journals are filled with articles that challenge assumptions about such supposedly human capacities as music making, grieving for our deceased loved ones, and ideas of fairness. About human beings and music, one scholar argues, "Music is far, far older than our

---

1. The need to take the sciences seriously is not only a Catholic concern; see James M. Gustafson, *An Examined Faith: The Grace of Self-Doubt* (Minneapolis: Fortress Press, 2004). This deceptively slim book is an invaluable resource for thinking about theology and nontheological disciplines.

2. See Thomas Aquinas, *Summa Theologiae* I, q. 78, a. 4.

3. Note that some traditions—e.g., Jainism, a very strict sect of Hinduism—emphasize the intrinsic value of *all* forms of life, including insects. See Baird Callicott, "Traditional American Indian and Western European Attitudes toward Nature: An Overview," *Environmental Ethics* 4, no. 4 (1982): 293–318; Christopher G. Farmarin, "Atman, Identity, and Emanation: Arguments for a Hindu Environmental Ethic," *Comparative Philosophy* 2, no. 1 (2011); and Po-keung Ip, "Taoism and the Foundations of Environmental Ethics," *Environmental Ethics* 5, no. 4 (1983): 335–43.

species."[4] There is evidence that some animals grieve for their dead—this is indeed the case with chimpanzees and elephants—and there is evidence as well that many animals have at least a rudimentary sense of justice and are also willing to share.[5]

Where the scientist might ask the question "What makes us unique as humans?" the theologian's question is "What makes human beings the image of God?" As I noted above, traditionally the answer to this question has rested with human rationality (Thomas Aquinas, Descartes). The classic Christian thinkers have assumed that human beings are alone among living creatures in their capacity to reason and to reflect on this reasoning. Yet locating human uniqueness in the abstract intellectual realm is no longer as widely held nor as well-grounded in human knowledge as it may have been in the time of Aquinas or Descartes. One contemporary thinker who has spent much time on this question is J. Wentzel van Huyssteen, whose reflections on this topic are both provocative and refreshing, if also controversial.[6]

In asking the question of the nature of the human, van Huyssteen is impatient with theological constructions that are abstract and that too easily dismiss the significance of human embodiment. We need, he says, to turn to the "earthy, embodied dimensions of humanness."[7] He dismisses disembodied ideas that "could easily float free above text, body, and nature in exotically baroque, overly abstract, metaphysical speculations."[8] Van Huyssteen notes that "the image of God is found not in some narrow intellectual or spiritual capacity, but in the whole

4. Natalie Angier, "Sonata for Humans, Birds, and Humpback Whales," *New York Times*, January 9, 2001, D5. The article notes that humpback whales use refrains that rhyme, and the hermit thrush "sings in the . . . pentatonic scale."

5. See, e.g., Frans B. M. de Waal, "Attitudinal Reciprocity in Food Sharing among Brown Capuchin Monkeys," *Animal Behaviour* 60, no. 2 (August 2000): 253–61; S. W. Griffiths and J. D. Armstrong, "Kin-Biased Territory Overlap and Food Sharing among Atlantic Salmon Juveniles," *Journal of Animal Ecology* 71, no. 3 (May 2002): 480–86; J. Moussaieff Masson and Susan McCarthy, *When Elephants Weep: The Emotional Lives of Animals* (New York: Delacorte Press, 1995); and Gerald S. Wilkinson, "Reciprocal Food Sharing in the Vampire Bat," *Nature* 208, no. 8 (March 1984).

6. J. Wentzel van Huyssteen, *Alone in the World? Human Uniqueness in Science and Theology*, The Gifford Lectures, University of Edinburgh, 2004 (Grand Rapids, MI: Eerdmans, 2006).

7. See van Huyssteen, "Theology, Science, and Human Nature," *The Princeton Seminary Bulletin* 27, no. 3 (2006): 201.

8. Van Huyssteen, *Alone in the World?* 273.

human being, 'body and soul.'"⁹ As we have seen with other philosophers and theologians on the topics already covered, human embodiment emerges yet again as an essential dimension of the human.

Van Huyssteen considers various ways that human "uniqueness"
has been described, including the use of language, the reality of vulnerability and dependence, moral capacities, and religious belief. For example, drawing on the philosopher Alasdair MacIntyre's work, van
Huyssteen rejects the idea that the use of language is the single key that
sets us apart from other animals. "Language," he writes, "ultimately is
deeply embedded in the communicative structures of the prelinguistic
history of our animal past."¹⁰ To try and pinpoint human uniqueness in
one particular area or capacity, such as language, is neither possible nor
desirable, although surely the human use of language is one of the many
dimensions of our particularity.

As any number of other theologians interested in the interface of
science and theology will argue, the problem with some scientific understandings of the human is that they tend to be reductionistic or
physicalistic; in other words, they claim to capture what is human by
calculating the sum of the various parts. It can be argued, for example,
that our desires and emotions are simply a result of our internal workings (hormones, neural connections): stimulate one part of the brain and
the result is elation; stimulate another and the result is depression. Certainly it is the case in the understanding of some so-called "mental"
disorders that the real cause is ultimately physiological, as in autism or
schizophrenia, which used to be blamed on inadequate mothering. This
is not to say that *all* "mental" or psychological disorders are neurological,
but it is the case that brain function is a significant factor in some of
them.¹¹ So we need to be suspicious, on the one hand, of ideas of the
person that seem to discount altogether the role of the body and, on the
other hand, of those that seem to reduce our humanness simply to
physical cause and effect.

Drawing on the phenomenologist Maurice Merleau-Ponty and the
theologian Edward Farley, among others, van Huyssteen wants to
ground any idea of human uniqueness thoroughly in its embodied dimension, noting that "the biological is a fact of individual human reality
along with the givenness, on another level, of our intersubjective and

---

9. Ibid., 274.
10. Ibid., 287.
11. I will note below the complex interplay of brain and body in certain cases.

social relationality, and that it is these various dimensions of being human that ultimately define the embodied human condition."[12] Human distinctiveness is a complex, multifaceted reality and is not reducible to one thing. He notes that the Christian tradition has always held that the notion of the *imago Dei* "does represent something that is at the very heart of the Christian tradition" but that there has never been "an unchanging identity" of what the *imago Dei* consists.[13] His point is to underscore his conviction that the *imago Dei* "emerg[ed] *from nature itself*," thus showing that "God used natural history for religion and for religious belief to emerge as a natural phenomenon."[14]

Rather than focus on a single, discrete, and ahistorical dimension of the (spiritual) uniqueness of the human person, then, van Huyssteen argues that the human being has "emerged biologically as a center of embodied self-awareness, consciousness, personal identity, and moral responsibility." He goes onto elaborate:

> Personhood, when richly conceived in terms of imagination, symbolic propensities, and cognitive fluidity, may enable theology also to revise its notion of the *imago Dei* as a concept that acknowledges our close ties to our sister species in the animal world while at the same time challenging us to rethink our own species specificity, and in that sense our difference from other species.[15]

What does this mean? For van Huyssteen, the religious dimension of being human, which is key to our humanness, emerged from within the very same process as did all of our other capacities. Symbolic thinking, artistic expression, beliefs about our origin and our destiny, awareness of good and evil that are related to our religious ideas—these are some of the distinct ways that we human beings reflect on our lives, but these capacities are dependent on the evolutionary process that has brought us to where we are now.

Human "uniqueness" is thus not to be found in some clearly identifiable trait that human beings have and other animals do not. Far from distinguishing itself or, worse, separating itself from other "human sciences" that try to delve more deeply into questions about the meaning

---

12. Van Huyssteen, *Alone in the World?* 278.
13. Ibid., 314.
14. Ibid., 322; emphasis in original.
15. Ibid., 321.

of being human, theology is obliged to remain in conversation with different fields of study. What theology *can* do is offer what van Huyssteen says is its unique capacity to ask questions about the human potential for hope in a world where human beings are the cause of both joy and tragedy.

In my view, scientific analyses of the human contribute to an ever-richer picture of our complexity and our relationship with the rest of creation. Being created "in the image of God" is not a static reality found in one discrete and identifiable part of ourselves. Rather, it is a dynamic process of opening ourselves to the world, caring for it as best we can with all of our abilities, and reflecting on our place in the world with both awe and lament. While the sciences can enrich our knowledge of ourselves and of the world around us considerably, theology, as a discipline that draws on many other fields of study, can ask questions of meaning and truth that go beyond scientists' purview.[16]

Animals and Human Beings

Human beings are not alone in our capacity to use tools and language, nor are we unique in our possession of a sense of self-awareness. There are many studies now available that show how complex the lives of the nonhuman animal world can be.[17] It is clear that other animals—and not just primates, our closest relatives—have evolved various dimensions of what scientists call a "social morality." That is, for animals to survive, they need to develop ways of cooperating with others in order for their family and kin groups to find food and mates and raise their young. Some sense of "fairness" is necessary for group survival. Is this more

16. Undoubtedly, there are some who question this assertion—notably, the "new atheists," whose view of religion is that it is simply superstition. For a sensitive reflection on the relation between theology and the sciences, see Gustafson, *An Examined Faith*, n. 1 above, and the theologians discussed below. The academic journal *Zygon* regularly publishes articles on the interface between religion and the sciences.

17. See, e.g., Marc Bekoff and Dale Jamieson, eds., *Interpretation and Explanation in the Study of Animal Behavior* (Boulder, CO: Westview, 1990); Marc Bekoff, "The Evolution of Animal Play, Emotions, and Social Morality: On Science, Theology, Spirituality, Personhood and Love," *Zygon* 36 (2001): 615–56; David DeGrazia, *Taking Animals Seriously: Mental Life and Moral Status* (Cambridge: Cambridge University Press, 1996); Jaak Panksepp, *Affective Neuroscience: The Foundations of Human and Animal Emotions* (Oxford: Oxford University Press, 1998); and Frans B. M. De Waal and Peter L. Tyack, *Animal Social Complexity: Intelligence, Culture, and Individualized Societies* (Cambridge, MA: Harvard University Press, 2003).

than just "instinct"? A number of ethologists[18] argue that it is, in the back-and-forth communication that takes place when some animals are welcomed in a group and some are not, as well as in the symmetry that goes on in animal play. This sense of "social morality" is certainly not the same thing as the kinds of principles and agreements that are found among human communities, but it is also not simply a mindless instinct that drives animals in their social behavior.

It is interesting to reflect on the potential for some kind of thought process, or even morality, among animals because of the many implications that follow. If we are to take seriously the point that we have emerged—and, no doubt, are still emerging—from a complex process that we call evolution, and if we are also to take seriously that we share many dimensions of our being with our nonhuman animal relatives, then we cannot discount the findings of scientists who question the clear line between human and nonhuman. The implications for such a thought experiment are far ranging. If we see all of creation, including animals, as simply means to our human ends, then we run the risk of ruling out their intrinsic value. Such a view would run counter to God's response to all of creation: "God looked at everything he had made, and he found it very good" (Gen 1:31).

Empathy is one of those qualities that is necessary for any rudimentary sense of morality: to be moral, one must be able to consider how one's actions may affect another and vice versa. A capacity for empathy does appear in many different animal species; ethologists and philosophers alike suggest that it is the basis for what will later develop in humans. Some ethologists suggest that the capacity for play among animals—primates, dogs, cats, birds—suggests that they have a basic sense of fairness, since play requires a kind of equality and reciprocity between or among the players.[19] Anyone who has ever had an animal companion, or especially more than one at the same time, is aware of the complexity and individuality that any dog or cat may demonstrate, how strong relationships can develop with them, and how much animals can teach us about ourselves. The Catholic tradition has, especially in the last century, emphasized the personhood of human beings, but some have questioned whether this personalism might do an injustice to the

18. Ethology is the study of animals.

19. See Marc Bekoff and John Alexander Byers, *Animal Play: Evolutionary, Comparative, and Ecological Perspectives* (Cambridge: Cambridge University Press, 1998); and Marc Bekoff, "Social Play Behaviors," *BioScience* 34, no. 4 (April 1984): 228–33.

world around us, with its focus primarily on the human.[20] When we stress human personhood, are we properly contextualizing this personhood in the natural world?

The interested reader is encouraged to take up further questions about the human-animal relationship. For example, some animal rights advocates make arguments for a kind of "personhood" to be bestowed upon animals.[21] And if our nonhuman animal companions are to be considered deserving of a set of "rights," then what do we make of human domestication and slaughter of animals for food? As we learn more about our own "animal" nature and all that we share with our fellow creatures, we need to give careful and critical thought to how our human uniqueness may in fact not be quite so unique and to ponder our responsibilities to the world we share with them. Such thinking does not negate the conviction that we are made in the image of God but rather presses us to take into consideration our relationship to the world around us.

Human Beings and the World around Us

The topic of ecology, and more specifically of global climate change, is a controversial one. Some prominent political leaders have charged that climate change is a "hoax" that scientists have invented in order to make money, despite the overwhelming evidence that it is a reality.[22] In most treatments of theological anthropology until recent years, it would have been unusual to find references to the ecosphere or to global climate change. But it is now impossible to consider the human being as isolated and apart from our natural environment. The very future of life on earth depends on whether or not we as human beings are willing to take responsibility for the ways that we interact with our natural surroundings and affect the nonhuman animal, plant, and mineral life on which we

---

20. William C. French, "Subject-Centered and Creation-Centered Paradigms in Recent Catholic Thought," *The Journal of Religion* 70, no. 1 (January 1990): 48–72.

21. See Marc Bekoff, *Minding Animals: Awareness, Emotions, and Heart* (Oxford: Oxford University Press, 2002); David DeGrazia, "Great Apes, Dolphins, and the Concept of Personhood," *The Southern Journal of Philosophy* 35 (1997); and Peter Singer, *In Defense of Animals* (New York: Blackwell, 1985).

22. Brad Plumer, "Despite Rick Perry, Consensus on Climate Change Keeps Strengthening," *The Washington Post*, August 23, 2011.

depend. In other words, ecological issues do have an important place in theological anthropology.[23]

A crucial point to be made is the *placing* of human beings in the world itself. In many traditional treatments of theological anthropology, the working assumption is that all human beings share a common human nature and also common issues of concern: religion, relationships, sexuality, rationality, ethics, community. In these traditional understandings, the lived context of these concerns is simply "there"—the world in which we live, a neutral reality that does not need further comment or elaboration. Only in the last few hundred years have human beings developed the technologies that have allowed us to gain power *over* much of nature, rather than being subject to forces beyond our control. Francis Bacon's comment that scientific discovery should be driven not just by the quest for intellectual enlightenment but also for "the relief of man's estate" is both indicative of his time and of a new attitude toward nature.[24]

Certainly the "forces of nature" are to be seriously reckoned with. 2011 was a year of unprecedented natural disasters: earthquakes, tsunamis, tornadoes, hurricanes, flooding, wildfires—and here I am only including natural events that in some way impacted the United States! Yet many scientists ask whether we may detect the hand of humanity in the particular ferocity of some of these events: Is global climate change, with increasing temperatures, affecting the strength of storms? Are we in part responsible for the wildfires that have decimated parts of the southwest United States? And ought we not to be concerned about other parts of the world that are faring much worse in this changing climate, such as sub-Saharan Africa, the South American rain forests, and the Arctic and Antarctic polar ice caps? We are not alone in the world, and the vast interrelationships among humans, animals, and the ecosphere are increasingly evident.

There are some theological resources from the Catholic tradition that can be supportive of a more sensitive approach to the ecosphere. Given Catholicism's rootedness in "nature," both empirically and theologically, at least the three following theologians deserve mention. Denis Edwards suggests that Karl Rahner's theology offers a perspective that can attune

23. See, e.g., Anne M. Clifford, "Feminist Perspectives on Science: Implications for an Ecological Theology of Creation," *Journal of Feminist Studies in Religion* 8, no. 2 (Fall 1992): 65–90.

24. Francis Bacon, *Advancement of Learning* (Chicago: Encyclopedia Britannica Great Books Series, 1952 [1605]).

us more readily to the environment. Edwards notes how Rahner continuously stresses the point that we encounter God in our experience in the world, not apart from it. As he notes, "Rahner holds that when we go out of ourselves to our world, in knowledge, love, and commitment, we find ourselves also open to the infinite mystery that transcends all objects of immediate experience."[25] Thus, global climate change can be seen "as the place of God."[26] And although Rahner did not specifically address the issues that we identify today as contributing to the global climate crisis, his approach is open to engaging them.

The work of the Swiss theologian Hans Urs von Balthasar, who, like Rahner, never specifically addressed global climate change, can also be brought to bear as a resource for a more theologically informed attitude toward the natural world. Throughout his life, Balthasar was critical of what he considered the modern, anthropocentric mentality that viewed the world instrumentally, as the place where human beings could do what they wanted. Balthasar's approach was, rather, "doxological" (from the Greek, "words of praise"), one that stressed a contemplative attitude toward God, others, and the world. Anthony C. Sciglitano writes that "the utilitarian and instrumental view of nature is nothing short of blasphemous, for it ignores the splendor of God's work and instead seeks self-centered exploitation, whether economic, ecological, or both. What Balthasar thinks is called for is a contemplative beholding of creation's sacramentality, its disinterested self-giving and fruitfulness, its radiant goodness."[27]

Bernard J. F. Lonergan, a Canadian Jesuit, is arguably the theologian best equipped to deal with the religious and ethical implications of the sciences. As Richard M. Liddy observes, "Lonergan was perhaps the most unabashedly 'scientific' of modern theologians, yet he was basically a theologian."[28] In a very helpful essay, Liddy describes Lonergan's schema of progress, decline, and redemption and shows how his method suggests the necessity of both scientific and theological responses to the climate crisis. Liddy shows how a convergence of scientific evidence of

---

25. Denis Edwards, "Climate Change and the Theology of Karl Rahner," in *Confronting the Climate Crisis: Catholic Theological Perspectives*, ed. Jame Schaefer (Milwaukee: Marquette University Press, 2011), 240.

26. Ibid., 249.

27. Anthony C. Sciglitano Jr., "Hans Urs von Balthasar and Deep Ecology: Towards a Doxological Ecology," in Schaefer, 295.

28. Richard M. Liddy, "Changing Our Minds: Bernard Lonergan and Climate Change," in Schaefer, 255.

climate change, the inevitability of denial and bias—what theologians call "sin"—and the potential for conversion and redemption call for a thoughtful and informed response to this crisis.[29]

A more adequate theological anthropology, sensitive to the ecosphere, questions whether we are really at the center of the universe. Recall how the earth-centered model of the cosmos was challenged with the availability of new technologies that showed the earth as just one planet among others revolving around the sun. We are at a similar point in how we understand our place in the cosmos. Ecotheologians remind us that our very existence is dependent on the world around us. Without adequate water, no life can survive, human or nonhuman. The use of fossil fuels for human technologies has had a marked effect on the climate. Rising temperatures are affecting land, sea, and air, are threatening water sources, the air we breathe, and the very existence of some species. No adequate theological anthropology can ignore the importance of the ways we think about our place in the world nor can it avoid the implications of a mistaken sense of disconnection between humans and the natural world.

Neuroscience and the Human

Neuroscience is an emerging field of study that focuses on the brain and nervous system.[30] It is an interdisciplinary field of study that draws on biology, chemistry, physics, medicine, computer science, mathematics, and psychology. The immense amount of knowledge gained from neuroscience in recent decades has contributed to an increasingly sophisticated understanding of how humans (and other living beings) process knowledge, experience emotion, and use language, to name just a few areas. As we have come to learn more and more about how our brains work, how they depend on our complex physiology—that is, how we function as complete embodied beings, not just brains on top of disconnected bodies—questions arise about the possibility of neuroscience being able to explain fully the dynamics of human beings. And it is not

---

29. Ibid.

30. For information on neuroscience, see the following resources: the Society for Neuroscience, www.sfn.org; The International Society for the History of Neurosciences Neuroscience Information Framework, http://neuinfo.org; also, a neuroscience tutorial created by Diana Weedman Molavi, PhD, at the Washington University School of Medicine is available at http://thalamus.wustl.edu/course.

just our "physical" capacities—that is, vision, hearing, perception, and so forth—that neuroscience explores. As I noted above, the fact that our moods are physiologically based has changed the ways that so-called mental illnesses are understood. While space and my lack of expertise do not allow for a full description of the findings of neuroscience here, I agree with Philip Clayton that "the neurosciences are now producing alternative explanatory candidates in the study of the human person."[31] That is to say, some scientists are increasingly confident that they will able—if not now, certainly in the future—to give a complete understanding of the human person. Philosophical and especially theological understandings, to the extent that they are grounded in some nonphysical basis for the human, such as rationality or the soul, no longer have any credibility, at least for some scientists, in an era when we are increasingly able to take the measure of the whole person with observable data.

How are theologians to respond? There is in fact a very lively debate among theologians and scientists going on today. While some scientists are immediately dismissive of anything religious, a number of theologians with scientific expertise are taking some of these findings very seriously.[32] Among them is Philip Clayton, who advances an argument both for theology taking scientific findings very seriously as well as for a more robust theological account of the person in response to scientific reductionism. "Scientific reductionism" essentially says that all that we can, or need, to know about the human person can be known by science, in measurable ways. This kind of reductionism is also sometimes known

31. Philip Clayton, "Neuroscience, the Person, and God: An Emergentist Account," *Zygon* 35, no. 3 (September 2000): 617.

32. Concerning the "new atheism" debate, see Terry Eagleton, *Reason, Faith, and Revolution: Reflections on the God Debate* (New Haven, CT: Yale University Press, 2009); and S. T. Joshi, *The Unbelievers: The Evolution of Modern Atheism* (Amherst, NY: Prometheus Books, 2011). For the primary texts of the "new atheism," see Richard Dawkins, *The God Delusion* (Boston: Houghton Mifflin, 2008); Daniel Clement Dennett, *Breaking the Spell: Religion as a Natural Phenomenon* (New York: Viking, 2006); Sam Harris, *The End of Faith: Religion, Terror, and the Future of Reason* (New York: W. W. Norton & Co., 2004); Christopher Hitchens, *God Is Not Great: How Religion Poisons Everything* (New York: Twelve, 2007); and Victor Stenger, *God the Failed Hypothesis: How Science Shows That God Does Not Exist* (Amherst, NY: Prometheus Books, 2007). For texts explicitly against "new atheism," see David Berlinski, *Devil's Delusion: Atheism and Its Scientific Pretensions* (New York: Crown Forum, 2008); Peter Hitchens, *Rage against God* (New York: Continuum, 2010); Ian S. Markham, *Against Atheism: Why Dawkins, Hitchens, and Harris Are Fundamentally Wrong* (Malden, MA: Wiley-Blackwell, 2010).

as "physicalism," where the physical is the measure of everything. On the whole, it is safe to say that those theologians who, like Clayton (including others such as the Roman Catholic theologian John Haught, John Polkinghorne, Arthur Peacocke, and Nancey Murphy), engage in dialogue with the sciences are convinced of the necessity of good science, find the theory of evolution to be convincing, and do not see an irreducible conflict between science and theology. And while not all of these theologians come to the same conclusions in responding to the sciences, they are all convinced that theology needs to take science very seriously. But, they conclude, science does not have all the answers and cannot fully or adequately explain the mystery of the human person.

Clayton argues for what he calls "emergent monism" and, as we shall see shortly, a corresponding "emergentist supervenience."[33] Monism, he argues, assumes the unity of nature. There is no "natural" sphere opposed to or alongside of a "supernatural" sphere: "the world is one . . . it constitutes a distinct order."[34] My understanding of Clayton is that this "monism" is not so much a denial of the transcendent character of life, in the traditional sense that Catholicism has understood the "natural" and the "supernatural," but rather a rejection of the kind of dualism that assumes a two-story universe, where the supernatural exists "up there" and we live "down here" in the natural world. Given this monistic framework, Clayton further argues that the "mental is dependent on, yet not reducible to, the physical."[35] In other words, the workings of our minds are entirely dependent on the fact that we have (physical) brains. This does not mean that our ideas and emotions are themselves simply physical, but that they *emerge* from our physicality. Clayton distinguishes between a sense of "personhood," with all that this implies (sociability, intentionality, intellectual reflection) and personhood's rootedness in its physical, organic location in our bodies. He points out that "personhood is therefore a level of analysis that has no complete translation into a state of the body or brain—no matter how complete our neuroscience might be."[36] There remains a level of explanation that cannot be reduced to scientific formulae; in other words, personhood cannot be reduced to the sum of its parts. Later in this article, Clayton defines his position as an "emergentist supervenience": "Simply

33. Clayton, "Neuroscience, the Person, and God," 643.
34. Ibid.
35. Ibid., 634.
36. Ibid., 630.

put, supervenience grants the dependence of mental phenomena on physical phenomena while at the same time denying the reducibility of the mental to the physical."[37]

There is, then, a nonreducibility of our personhood to our physical/neurological makeup: who we are, Clayton and others argue, *emerges from* the physical but—to use a philosophical and theological term—*transcends* the physical. Thus, theologians should not ignore neuroscience, nor should they see it as an enemy or as offering a view of the human that must be resisted. Rather, they should engage neuroscience in conversation. This will allow for a fuller understanding of ourselves and our complexity while still maintaining that there is a dimension to personhood that goes beyond its physicality.

But here the reader might object: But doesn't this simply say that there is "something more" but that it can't be observed or explained?[38] For what reason ought an intelligent person to think that science cannot provide us with sufficient answers? And what is this "something more"? To this question, John Haught argues that our very capacity to think and reflect on our own knowledge and the necessity to trust in this capacity is "proof" enough. He asks, "Is the essentially mindless, impersonal and purposeless universe entailed by evolutionary naturalism resourceful enough to explain and ground, in an ultimate sense, the trust you are in fact placing in your own critical intelligence at this moment?"[39] That is to say, the very fact that someone is attending to evidence, thinking about what it means, and trying to make it intelligible is itself an indication that the "impersonal and purposeless" workings of the physical world are not a sufficient description of this very world or of the persons who live in it. Haught is indebted to Bernard Lonergan's "transcendental imperatives"—be attentive, be intelligent, be reasonable, be responsible—which he uses as a response to one who would doubt the human capacity to trust in the very cognitional processes that make scientific investigation possible.

As a theologian, I may not know the details of the neuroscientist's findings; I would need highly specialized training even to understand

---

37. Ibid., 632.

38. See Gustafson, *An Examined Faith*, 18–34, for a very helpful imaginative description of how a college student might deal with all of the various scientific and humanistic disciplines and what questions might emerge.

39. John Haught, "Theology, Evolution, and the Human Mind: How Much Can Biology Explain?" *Zygon* 44, no. 4 (December 2009): 926.

them adequately. But I am glad that there are neuroscientists probing the complexities of our brains. It is good to know that there are causes and real or potential treatments for a number of illnesses previously thought to be "mental." We are all aware of how our "state of mind" can be affected by temperature, daylight, diet, and exercise. Women in their fertile years are often able to make sense out of their moodiness by considering what time of the month it is. So knowing more about how our brains work is not insignificant for the theologian. It may in time even potentially enrich our theologies of sin and grace.

Technology, Medicine, and the Human Person

Perhaps the scientific advances that are most evident to many of us are those that touch our own lives—those having to do with medical advances, treatment of diseases, and life at its earliest beginnings and at the very end. The field of bioethics, broadly speaking, attempts to reflect on the values that are at stake when decisions must be made about the morality of some treatments or technologies (e.g., in vitro fertilization [IVF], treatment of persons who are in persistent vegetative states, gender reassignment surgery, etc.). Bioethics is a complex and extensive area of study, and I can only touch on some of the issues with which a theological anthropology is concerned.[40]

In a very helpful book of essays on theological anthropology and medical ethics, Roberto Dell'Oro comments, "At present, the field of bioethics seems to exhibit a certain resistance to the integration of theological voices, a methodological 'closure' of sorts that might appear as both unexpected and startling to an attentive observer of the field's beginnings."[41] Dell'Oro notes that much ethical discussion on bioethical issues of public significance—that is, issues that go beyond a confessional dimension—seems to avoid any question of "ultimate" significance in favor of a more pragmatic approach that seeks moral consensus. The

40. For a theological perspective on bioethics, see Lisa Sowle Cahill, *Theological Bioethics: Participation, Justice, and Change* (Washington, DC: Georgetown University Press, 2005); Earl E. Shelp, *Secular Bioethics in Theological Perspective* (Boston: Kluwer Academic Publishers, 1996); and James J. Walter and Thomas A. Shannon, *Contemporary Issues in Bioethics: A Catholic Perspective* (Lanham, MD: Rowman & Littlefield Publishers, 2005).

41. Roberto Dell'Oro, "Theological Anthropology and Bioethics," in *Health and Human Flourishing: Religion, Medicine, and Moral Anthropology*, ed. Carol Taylor and Roberto Dell'Oro (Washington, DC: Georgetown University Press, 2006), 14.

question then becomes, what does a *Christian* theological anthropology contribute to these complex questions? What sort of understanding of the person informs our decision making on both difficult issues and more "everyday" issues?

Does a Christian perspective make a difference? It should not be a surprise that my view is that it should. When a Christian is faced with taking a course of action regarding some form of medical technology and human life, certain fundamental convictions need to be front and center. Here I will draw both from theological ethicist Margaret Farley and from the widely accepted key principles of Catholic social teaching. In this section, I am necessarily straddling the boundary between theology and ethics.

Margaret Farley writes that there is strong agreement among medical ethicists that certain themes are key: autonomy, nonmaleficence, beneficence, and justice.[42] She observes that of all these themes, autonomy has emerged, especially in the modern era, as the most prominent. She comments, "The central ethical requirement to respect persons is frequently considered identical with the requirement to respect the autonomy— the self-determining, self-governing, decision-making capacity—of persons".[43] Yet in recent years, the priority of autonomy has come under criticism, and not only in the area of medical ethics. In particular, feminist ethicists like Farley have asked whether autonomy should be seen as *the* main characteristic of human persons. This is not to question the value of autonomy, since it is crucial for people, women especially, to have the power to make decisions for themselves. But holding autonomy as the highest value can obscure the fact that none of us is born autonomous; that is, we are all born into conditions of dependence and often end our lives in dependence, completely reliant on relationships, either intimate or professional. The fact that human beings cannot survive without relationships needs to be stressed as well. Early feminist ethicists emphasized an "ethic of care"; that is, rather than view the human person as primarily one who makes rational moral decisions, some feminist ethicists argued that the person—again, particularly women—sees herself

---

42. These are taken from Margaret Farley, *Compassionate Respect: A Feminist Approach to Medical Ethics and Other Questions*, 2002 Madeleva Lecture in Spirituality (Mahwah, NJ: Paulist Press, 2002), 25.

43. Ibid., 26. See also J. B. Schneewind, *The Invention of Autonomy: A History of Modern Moral Philosophy* (New York and Cambridge: Cambridge University Press, 1998).

as primarily connected to others and makes decisions accordingly.[44] Farley argues that we do not have to choose between these two values— *both* autonomy *and* relationality are central to being human and to making moral decisions. These two values connect with much that is central in Christian theology: that each person possesses intrinsic dignity and that each person exists in a community of persons.

The principles of Catholic social teaching (CST) paint a larger picture of the human person in community.[45] Especially worth emphasizing are CST's focus on the community and the common good, the option for the poor and vulnerable, and solidarity. What CST stresses is that all human beings have certain rights and responsibilities, that these are exercised not just individually but within a communal context, and that we must care especially for the poor and vulnerable. The common good is good for all of us; it is never right to put individual goods above the good of the whole.

Yet in contemporary North American culture, the complementary values of both autonomy and relationality, as well as the significance of the common good, seem to be in short supply. The desires of human beings for just about any consumer product they want—desires that by definition will never be fulfilled, since the system works by continuously coming up with new products—seem to suggest that the central moral compass for human beings is in what makes someone "feel good."[46] A Christian perspective on medical treatments and technologies should always hold the good of the *whole* person as the highest value, as that person exists in community and in relation to God.

44. See Carol Gilligan, *In a Different Voice: Psychological Theory and Women's Development* (Cambridge, MA: Harvard University Press, 1982).

45. For the major themes of Catholic social teaching, see Office for Social Justice St. Paul and Minneapolis online at http://osj.webaloo.com/major_themes.aspx. For a more in-depth treatment with quotations from church documents, see the National Conference of Catholic Bishops United States Catholic Conference online at http://nccbuscc.org/sdwp/catholicteachingprinciples.shtml. And for the complete Vatican Compendium of the Social Doctrine of the Church online, visit http://www.vatican.va/roman_curia/pontifical_councils/justpeace/documents/rc_pc_justpeace_doc_20060526_compendio-dott-soc_en.html.

46. On desire, see Vincent J. Miller, *Consuming Religion: Christian Faith and Practice in a Consumer Society* (New York and London: Continuum, 2004); on "feeling good," see David Brooks, "If It Feels Right . . . ," *New York Times*, September 12, 2011, http://www.nytimes.com/2011/09/13/opinion/if-it-feels-right.html?_r=1&ref=davidbrooks.

It would take a library of books to address adequately the many questions that bioethics raises for theological anthropology. But it is possible here to suggest some theological principles that can inform our thinking and make a few comments as to how these might be relevant to some of the questions involving science, technology, and the person. The first point is to reiterate that human beings are made in the image of God. Although it is difficult to locate the *imago Dei* in any single dimension of the person, such as our rationality, we are called to consider how we live this out in our lives. The Christian trinitarian understanding of God as Creator, Redeemer, and Sustainer suggests that as cocreators, we have a responsibility to all of creation to assist in making the world a place of God's presence; to heal ourselves, each other, and the world with God's help; and to help maintain the world's ongoing life and flourishing. How does our being in the image of God inform our decisions about reproductive technologies? Our consumer-oriented culture assumes that if we want something, we should be able to buy it. Does this mean that we should be able to buy whatever it takes to have a child or to ensure that we have a child of the right sex? Ought we to consider how these technologies and treatments affect our dignity as persons and the dignity of those who come after us? Are there ways of being creative and nurturing that might not involve having our own biological children? My point here is not to denigrate the many medical advances that have been developed to treat infertility. Many of these technologies are a blessing to people and have increased our knowledge of reproduction considerably. But they do not come without a cost, personally, financially, or theologically. An adequate theology of human beings as cocreators with God will be highly sensitive to the potential risks of "playing God."

Second, the Christian tradition is grounded in God's free act of love in becoming human, making our embodiment the privileged place of God's revelation. We might ask how a thoughtful and prayerful incarnational sense informs how we treat our bodies, which are by definition mortal. The paschal mystery is at the center of our Christian faith, but this does not mean than death is simply an inconvenience on the way to resurrection. The fear of death is part of what makes us human; suicide is, among other things, a tragic statement that means one finds death preferable to the pain of living. How do our attitudes about death and our willingness to take part in the paschal mystery affect the way we understand our inevitably growing, changing, and aging bodies? We live in a culture that glorifies youth and certain narrow standards of beauty. How ought a Christian to approach cosmetic surgery? While we have an obligation to care for ourselves and our bodies—to eat well, to exercise, to enjoy the blessings of the earth—we will all die, in dependent old age or in some other way. How can we embrace our embodiment as Christians? How can we age and die with grace and dignity?

Even more, a Christian sensitivity to our finitude and mortality should be aware of our tendencies to see only what we want to see, to avoid considering how our actions affect others or the wide world, and to act for our own gain at the expense of others'. In other words, our sinfulness is a necessary consideration. As feminist ethicists have noted, sinfulness does not always show itself as pride. It can also be found in a refusal to be one's full self, in an unwillingness to engage in moral deliberation. It can be easier to "follow the crowd," yet, as Lonergan reminds us, we need to be aware of the sorts of biases that creep into our thinking and cloud our vision.

Third, we live not alone but with and among others: spouses, children, coworkers, fellow citizens, and the rest of the world. As Christians, we have an obligation to care for the most vulnerable among us. And, as I have stressed above, human dignity is located not only in our brains but in our entire being. Do we ensure that the many resources available to treat illnesses and to make lives better are available to as many people as possible? In the United States, unlike nearly every other country in the "developed" world, health care is a market commodity. Catholic health institutions have for centuries been places where the poor and most vulnerable are able to find care. In trying economic times, however, these hospitals, clinics, and health centers find themselves squeezed as much as other institutions. What is an adequate *Christian* approach to resources for health care? And how is this approach negotiated in a country with diverse religious traditions and attitudes?

These are just some of the questions that need to be addressed in a Christian understanding of the human person. The Catholic tradition has no shortage of opinions on various bioethical questions. My point here is that the larger picture of how we understand ourselves needs to inform the ways we answer these questions.

Conclusion

We live in a world of dizzying technological and scientific innovation. As I have been writing this book, news articles have appeared that suggest that young people have an ability to multitask that older people lack; that playing video games helps to develop the skills that would benefit (future) airplane pilots; that Google is "making us stupid"; that drug treatments may help to halt the advance of Alzheimer's disease; that very early testing for determining the sex of a fetus is now available. The list can go on and on. By the time this book appears, there will no doubt be more scientific advances to note.

The Christian cannot simply stand by and ignore these issues. They all raise theological questions. Indeed, they *demand* theological responses. My effort here has been to take these scientific and technological advances as seriously as possible and to consider how we might respond. And in our responding, we need to be careful, on the one hand, not to fall back into a simplistic religious fundamentalism that finds a pat answer (from the Bible, the tradition, or the *Catechism*) or, on the other hand, to say simply that religion and science are two different fields (which they are) and that there is no possibility of their meeting. These issues are complex and demand a complex response. As I noted in chapter 6, engaging difficult moral and scientific issues involves a willingness to grapple with complexity and to do the hard work that such grappling requires.

The human desire to know, which I have highlighted in this chapter, brings both blessings and conundrums. Science offers many answers, but it does not ask all the questions that need to be asked. The Christian theological tradition offers rich resources for thoughtful and prayerful deliberation, from our relationships with our domestic animal companions to our place on earth.

Conclusion

Seeking Light and Beauty

Are we really "spirit(s) seeking light and beauty"? Or are we better described in other terms that might reveal more of our dark and sinful sides? As a Catholic, I maintain a basic and stubborn optimism about the human person, but any careful reading of the tradition provides ample material for a much less sunny estimation. Our journey through the tradition and some recent challenges to Christian understandings of the person have provided what I hope is a thoughtful and realistic picture of the complexity of what it means to be human. It is also a picture that is necessarily incomplete. In writing this book, I have become even more aware of how much there is to say about theological anthropology and how difficult it is to do justice to this immense topic in a short book.

The topic of theological anthropology is complex, drawing on what the Scriptures and the tradition have to say, as well as on what we have come to know through various disciplines and through our own experiences. My approach has been to use what David Tracy refers to as a "critical correlation" of sources. On the one hand, there is what Tracy calls the "Christian fact," with all that it encompasses: Scripture, tradition, church teachings, papal documents—in short, the whole complex of what we have inherited in our religious tradition. In the first three chapters, I drew on this tradition to bring out the anthropological issues that emerged again and again in the tradition.

On the other hand, there is what Tracy refers to as "common human experience," meaning that complex of practices and ideas that constitutes both our everyday and our more extraordinary lives.[1] As Tracy sees it,

---

1. David Tracy, *Blessed Rage for Order: The New Pluralism in Theology* (New York: Crossroad, 1975). I was a student of Tracy's in the late 1970s.

the task of theology is to put these two sources into a "mutually critical correlation" in which both pose questions to each other and propose possible answers. My appropriation of this method has been to put Christian teaching about the human in conversation with some of the theological, philosophical, and scientific issues that have emerged in the present.

Since the publication of Tracy's book over thirty-five years ago, the idea that human experience is "common" has, as I suggested in chapter 4, come under a great deal of criticism as the diversity of human experiences has become more widely known and appreciated. "Experience" itself is a fraught term, and it has been used rather too widely and without sufficient attention to the differences that we Westerners sometimes ignore. I would agree, however, with the late Edward Schillebeeckx that there are indeed some "anthropological constants" that, despite immense cultural differences, persist in human life, no matter where or when it is lived.

There are a number of important dimensions of theological anthropology that have not been specifically addressed in this book, such as spirituality and sacramental life. Nor have I discussed at length what it means to know that we are mortal and wonder about life beyond death or how our desire for beauty finds itself expressed in the arts and in other dimensions of life. My interests here have been in our Christian theological anthropological inheritance, the wisdom it offers us, and how we might approach certain pressing questions in the present. What does it mean to live in a fragmented age? How do we sort out what it means to be male, female, gay, young, old, lesbian, transgender, or disabled, desiring others in love and for mutual pleasure and for shared life? Given the monumental terrors that humans have wreaked on the earth in the last century, not to mention in the more distant past, how can we respond? And given the advances in science and technology, how do we understand ourselves as created in the image of God in a time when we seem to have the power to take life in our own hands?

But even more seriously, we need to ask ourselves what difference it means for us *as Christians* to be human beings. One of the ways this question gets asked in the present is through the bumper sticker slogan "What would Jesus do?" Would he drive a Hummer, a Prius, or, perhaps more likely, not drive at all? How would he respond to the global climate crisis? Instead of giving sermons to large crowds of people, would he Twitter or blog? Simply inserting "Jesus" into the present raises many more questions than it answers, but it can be an interesting experiment.

I have tried to present some of the complexity of the Christian message about what it means to be human and how it is impossible to come up with easy answers to complicated questions.

The great Jewish writer Elie Wiesel tells the story of the pious Jew who looks around the world, sees all the good and the evil that human beings do, and exclaims, "The world is in such terrible shape! Why has the Messiah not yet come?" And the pious Christian stands beside the pious Jew and says, "The Messiah has come. So, why is the world in such terrible shape?" In another story, in Wiesel's famous novel *Night*, the rabbis at a concentration camp put God on trial, find him guilty, and then gather together afterward to pray. Somehow, despite evil and terror, human beings continue to find strength and hope and even beauty in their faith. My conviction is that deep within us is a desire for meaning and hope for our fragile lives, a hunger for something "more" that cannot be fulfilled with "stuff," with electronic gadgets, or even in another person. Our hungers, as Rahner would say, are ultimately supernatural and existential.

Hans Urs von Balthasar, a Swiss theologian whose focus on theological aesthetics has been very influential in recent years, argued throughout his life that theology needs to recover a sense of the great transcendentals: truth, goodness, and beauty. Truth, he lamented, had become something to be measured or proven; its luminosity and richness had been lost in a modern quest for certainty. Goodness was no longer a full life of virtue but was now reduced to correct decision making and right conduct. And beauty—alas, beauty had been exiled from the sphere of serious thought and reduced to ornamentation and the superficially pretty.

While I strenuously disagree with Balthasar on a number of issues, including his conceptions of the roles of women and of offices in the church, his call to retrieve truth, goodness, and beauty not only in theology but even more so in human life suggests a way of bringing a number of things together in concluding this book. Human beings do indeed seek truth, goodness, and beauty. And in the Christian tradition, we do not always find them where we think they ought to be: we find truth in stories and parables, we find goodness in failure, we find beauty in the cross.

The desire to know is one of the main themes of the first story we read in the Bible. The knowledge that the first couple in this foundational myth come to is "the knowledge of good and evil," and it turns out to be their apparent downfall. But without this desire and this knowledge, what would we have? The world of Eden, from the other side of the Fall, looks rather bland and dull. The desire to know fuels our stories, from the ancient Israelites to the disciples in search of the truth: "Master, to whom shall we go? You have the words of eternal life" (John 6:68). The early theologians desired to know and communicate the truth, and this led them to use philosophical terms from pagan thinkers to make sense of their beliefs, drawing on the concepts of their own time. Augustine and Anselm both saw the theological task as "faith seeking under-standing" and were convinced that this desire to know their faith would lead them closer to God. The Reformation and Enlightenment figures we explored also sought the truth—and along the way, some of them also narrowed the meaning of truth. We have inherited this Enlighten-ment sense that the only true thing is what can be proven or demon-strated, yet who among us has not learned something deeply true in poetry, a novel, a great work of art? In a relationship? In nature? And postmodern thinkers argue that we need to expose the reality—shall we say the truth?—of our situation, which is one of multiplicity and fragmentation.

In the present, seeking the truth is as complicated as it ever was. We have more access to information than ever before: with a click of a mouse we can find out just about anything we need to know, from how to say something in another language to whether or not the person one is dat-ing is who he or she claims to be. But these fragmentary answers seldom give us the sense of finality and resolution that we seek. We spend much of our time getting more information but knowing less about ourselves, others, and the meaning that we seek. The tradition we inherit has a great deal of wisdom to impart about how human beings in the past have sought the truth. My hope is that readers will be interested enough to explore some of these great thinkers further, in their own words.

The search for goodness is also a story we have followed. Early Chris-tians, we are told, lived in common and shared all their goods (Acts 2:44). Christianity has constantly emphasized the need to care for the poor, the oppressed, the downtrodden, those on the margins of society. The earliest Christians developed a "rule of faith" that sustained them in their daily lives. Benedict and the monastic tradition developed a distinctive way of life for those willing to give up the expected path of marriage and family for a "more narrow way" that involved poverty, chastity, obedi-ence, and life in a community. Thomas Aquinas emphasized the devel-opment of virtue on the part of the devout Christian and provided a model for moral theology that continues well into the present. One could say that the Reformation thinkers saw their task as returning the Christian tradition to its origins, which, with good reason, they saw as having been lost when the institutional church gained political power. One of their signal contributions was to make the case that every Christian—male, female, ordained, or lay—had a vocation from God and that we were all bound to follow this call, whether it led to marriage or, more rarely, to vowed religious life. Enlightenment thinkers sought freedom of thought but also ideas of equality, as did nineteenth-century abolitionists and suffragists and twentieth-century liberation movements. The search for economic, racial, and gender justice continues in our own time. The economic crisis of the latter part of the first decade of the twenty-first century has raised the question of justice anew. Is it just that some people can make millions from betting on the vagaries of the market system? Is it just that corporations can profit from moving their manufacturing to other parts of the world because of lower labor costs? And, to connect this with the issue of the truth, are we morally obligated to tell the truth in all situations in life?

While some argue that the world is actually becoming a better place than it ever was (as Steven Pinker claims in *The Better Angels of Our Nature*[2]), we still face enormous injustices, both personal and social. The Christian vision of goodness takes its inspiration from the parables of Jesus and the great eschatological vision of Matthew 25, stories that envisioned a great banquet where the least were seated at the head of the table and the Prodigal Son was welcomed home with a lavish party. If some of the visions of goodness that the parables communicate strike us as offensive—I have always tended to empathize with the elder son, not the Prodigal, and to take issue with the vineyard owner paying all his employees the same wage, no matter how long they worked—then we have heard them correctly and need to consider how it is that our own practices of goodness ought to take shape. What are our obligations to those in countries who experience the fallout from European and American market decisions? What of our obligations to the natural world, to future generations? In all of these crucial issues, having the right kind of information is essential—that is, goodness must be connected with the truth—but information alone will not guarantee that one's decision is morally right. Christian traditions of prayer and meditation, knowledge of church teaching, and participation in a Eucharistic

---

2. Steven Pinker, *The Better Angels of Our Nature* (New York: Viking, 2011).

community all help in the formation of a good conscience, which is the obligation of every Christian.

And finally, the search for beauty takes on many forms. Anselm was delighted by the beauty of human reason and its correspondence with revelation. Julian of Norwich saw the poignant beauty of the loyal servant who falls and fails in his eagerness to please his master. Thomas Aquinas saw all of creation in one great cosmic order of emanation from and return to God. The beauty of the great medieval cathedrals, the works of artists like Michelangelo and Rembrandt, the magnificent music of Bach and Messaien, and the poetry of Dante, Hopkins, and Anne Sexton express in architecture, visual art, music, and poetry what cannot be said in ordinary prose. Art shows us how to see or hear or speak something that opens up a dimension of reality that cannot be found in more mundane ways. Von Balthasar argued that only in the beauty of the cross is God's glory fully revealed. These traditional ideas of beauty were closely correlated with a sense of truth and goodness. In the present, we might ask how our search for beauty is also connected with goodness and truth.

We have now what is known as a "beauty industry" that provides us with a constant barrage of images of how we should look and act and tells us that any sign of aging or any extra flesh should be eliminated with the (new and improved!) products that we can buy. As other observers of the contemporary scene have observed, even religion has been brought into the nexus of consumerism.[3] Our images of what is beautiful are shaped by an industry that survives by constantly changing these images—although one might say that the basic ideal is young, slim, wealthy, and white—and prompting us to buy products to emulate and possess them. We find ourselves trying to keep up with constantly changing and better ways of presenting ourselves to the world. There is a heightened awareness of the power of this industry on the part of feminist writers and ecologists concerned about the never-ending cycle of purchasing and discarding and its impact on the environment, not to mention its impact on our personal and social lives.

But I do not think the Christian solution is to live a life of total austerity, owning only a few changes of clothing, eating simply for nourish-

---

3. See, e.g., Vincent J. Miller, *Consuming Religion: Christian Faith and Practice in a Consumer Culture* (New York and London: Continuum, 2004); and John Kavanaugh, *Following Christ in a Consumer Society: The Spirituality of Cultural Resistance* (Maryknoll, NY: Orbis Books, 2006 [1981]).

ment, avoiding the arts and culture, and, in general, eschewing any aesthetic dimension to life—perhaps living a life somewhat like John the Baptist's! The oft-quoted remark by the character Shug in Alice Walker's novel *The Color Purple* comes to mind: "I think it pisses God off if you walk by the color purple in a field somewhere and don't notice it."[4] Rather, we need to be aware of the choices we make and exercise our rational and moral capacities to see that beauty is a quality that, at its best, inclines the person to share it and ultimately can help lead to a better world. Beauty has a potential for hospitality that is not sufficiently recognized in contemporary culture where it is too often reduced to a shallow impression of its forgotten depth.

The human desire for beauty is a desire for order and harmony at times, but it is also a desire for variety, newness, vastness, delicacy, humor, and hope. Our desires for beauty are one dimension of our desires for the infinite. Beauty gives us a small share—in a poem, an icon, a song, a tree—that hints at the One who invites us to know, love, and enjoy all the riches that this incomprehensible Mystery offers us everywhere we look. We find this beauty in culture and in the arts, to be sure, but also in our relationships, in the world around us, in our animal companions, in a spiderweb outside our door. What beauty does is invite us to attend more closely to the mystery of our existence. It shows itself to us in ways that draw us in and delight us. A beautiful novel or poem or painting can also reveal great truths to us and suggest a way to live. Henri Nouwen's beautiful meditation on Rembrandt's painting *The Prodigal Son* is an example of how a work of art's beauty connects powerfully with truth and goodness.[5]

Rachel Shteir concludes an essay on academic studies of beauty by saying, "Beauty is anarchic, a force of nature, a gift. Like love, it is mysterious, not least of all because it can change your life."[6] While this author's focus is largely on standards of beauty as they apply to women, her point is also valid for our purposes here. Beauty stands first and foremost on its own, and, as Shteir comments, it is a gift. But what do we do with this gift? We can ignore it, abuse it, cheapen it, throw it away. Or we can allow it to open up otherwise hidden dimensions of our lives.

4. Alice Walker, *The Color Purple* (New York: Pocket Books, 1990), 203.

5. Henri Nouwen, *The Return of the Prodigal Son* (New York: Image Books, 1994). I am indebted to Dan Hartnett, SJ, for sharing this book with me some years ago.

6. Rachel Shteir, "Taking Beauty's Measure," *The Chronicle of Higher Education*, December 13, 2011.

My suggestion is that beauty ties into our deepest desires and, along with our desires for truth and goodness, can help us to know, love, and appreciate the Mystery who calls all of us.

Readers of this book are invited to consider their own desires for truth, goodness, and beauty and to think about where they might converge or diverge with some of these ideas. I encourage readers to delve deeply into the classic sources upon which this book has drawn as well as into some of the more recent works that comment on them or provide more contemporary visions of being human. Most of all, I hope that this book provides an opportunity to reflect on the mystery of being human, on our deepest desires, and on how the Christian tradition offers us rich and immense resources for this lifelong task.

Index